In-Memory Data Management Research

Series Editor

Prof. Dr. Dr. h.c. Hasso Plattner
Hasso Plattner Institute
Potsdam, Germany

For further volumes:
http://www.springer.com/series/11642

Matthieu-P. Schapranow

Real-time Security Extensions for EPCglobal Networks

Case Study for the Pharmaceutical Industry

 Springer

Dr.-Ing. Matthieu-P. Schapranow
Hasso Plattner Institute
Potsdam
Germany

ISBN 978-3-642-36342-9   ISBN 978-3-642-36343-6   (eBook)
DOI 10.1007/978-3-642-36343-6
Springer Heidelberg New York Dordrecht London

Library of Congress Control Number: 2013934271

Printed on acid-free paper

Springer is part of Springer Science+Business Media (www.springer.com)

Acknowledgments

I thank Prof. Dr. Hasso Plattner for supporting my research work for this dissertation by sharing countless inspiring thoughts and discussions during the course of my work. In addition, I thank Jürgen Müller and Martin Lorenz for collaboratively building student lectures, productive conversations, and many hints that lead to new insights. Moreover, I thank all my colleagues at the research chair at the Hasso Plattner Institute and at the SAP for involving me in numerous inspiring and innovative projects from academia and industry. I also thank all my friends for their understanding and long-lasting support that gave me the opportunity to take my time for performing my research activities and writing this dissertation.

I cannot finish without thanking my family for building a powerful environment to perform my research work. Especially, I thank Katrin for her loving encouragement, her constant stimulus to stay on track, and her support to complete this dissertation. I love you.

Ultimately, I would not have been able to finish my work without all your personal support. Thank you all for accompanying me during this important phase of my life.

Contents

Abbreviations

ACC	Access Control Client
ACL	Access Control List
ACS	Access Control Server
AD	Active Directory
ALE	Application Level Events
AM	Amplitude Modulation
B	Byte (8 Bit)
b	Bit
CA	Certificate Authority
CP	Certificate Profile
CPU	Central Processing Unit
CRL	Certificate Revocation List
CRM	Customer Relationship Management
CSR	Certificate Signing Request
DAC	Discretionary Access Control
DCI	Discovery Configuration and Initialization
DDoS	Distributed Denial-of-Service
DDR3	Double Data Rata Type 3
DES	Data Encryption Standard
EAN	Electronic Article Number
EC	European Commission
EC2	Elastic Computing Cloud
EPC	Electronic Product Code
EPCDS	Electronic Product Code Discovery Services
EPCIS	Electronic Product Code Information Services
ERP	Enterprise Resource Planning
EU	European Union
FFC	Far Field Communication
FM	Frequency Modulation
FMC	Fundamental Modeling Concepts
FOSSTRAK	Free and Open Source Software for Track and Trace
GB	Gigabyte (10^9 Byte)
Gb	Gigabit (10^9 Bit)

GHz	Gigahertz (10^9 Hz)
GS1	Global Standards 1
GT	Gigatransactions (10^9 Transactions)
HBAC	History-Based Access Control
HF	High Frequency
Hz	Hertz $\left[\frac{1}{s}\right]$
IFF	Identification Friend or Foe
IM	Inventory Management
ISIC	International Standard Industrial Classification
ISM	Industrial Scientific and Medical
ISO	International Standards Organization
IT	Information Technology
kB	Kilobyte (10^3 Byte)
kHz	Kilohertz (10^3 Hz)
KPI	Key Performance Indicator
LDAP	Lightweight Directory Access Protocol
LF	Low Frequency
LLRP	Low Level Reader Protocol
LW	Long Wave
MAC	Media Access Control
MHz	Megahertz (10^6 Hz)
MITM	Man-in-the-Middle
ms	Millisecond (10^{-3} s)
MW	Medium Wave
MW	Micro Wave
NDAC	Non-Discretionary Access Control
NFC	Near Field Communication
NIST	National Institute of Standards and Technology
ODRL	Open Digital Rights Language
ONS	Object Name Service
OTP	One-Time Password
PAP	Policy Administration Point
PDP	Policy Decision Point
PEP	Policy Enforcement Point
PET	Privacy Enhancing Technology
PIP	Policy Information Point
PKI	Public Key Infrastructure
PRN	Pseudo Random Number
PUF	Physical Uncloneable Function
PW	Password
PZN	Pharmazentralnummer (Central Pharmaceutical Number)
QPI	Intel's Quick Path Interconnect
RBAC	Role-Based Access Control
RDIMM	Registered Dual-Inline Memory Module

RFID	Radio Frequency Identification
RM	Reader Management
RSA	Rivest, Shamir, and Adleman Algorithm
RuBAC	Rule-Based Access Control
s	Second
SaaS	Software-as-a-Service
SGLN	Serialized Global Location Number
SGTIN	Serialized Global Trade Item Number
SHA	Secure Hash Algorithm
SHF	Super High Frequency
SME	Small and Midsize Enterprise
SOAP	Simple Object Access Protocol
SoD	Separation of Duties
SSCC	Serial Shipping Container Code
SSL	Secure Sockets Layer
SW	Short Wave
TCP	Transmission Control Protocol
TDS	Tag Data Standard
TDT	Tag Data Translation
TRS	Trust Relationship Server
UDP	User Datagram Protocol
UHF	Ultra High Frequency
URL	Unified Resource Locator
USA	United States of America
VPN	Virtual Private Network
WORM	Write-Once Read-Many
XACML	eXtensible Access Control Markup Language
XML	eXtensible Markup Language
XSLT	eXtensible Stylesheet Language Transformation

Figures

Tables

Listings

About the Book

The number of detected counterfeits at the borders of the European Union (EU) increases steadily. Counterfeits of exclusive and expensive goods are ranked highest, e.g., pharmaceutical goods [1]. Instead of using current identification techniques working on product classes, such as the Electronic Article Number (EAN), new identification methods working on item level, such as the Electronic Product Code (EPC), create the foundation of fine-grained tracking and tracing of individual goods [2]. Appropriate techniques for automatic reading of product data, such as Radio Frequency Identification (RFID), instead of one-dimensional bar codes, can improve handling of goods. As a result, a product's unique identity can be read automatically by passing it through reading gates. The gathered data can be verified and synchronized with enterprise applications, such as Enterprise Resource Planning (ERP) systems. For this purpose, the product's identity, date and time of the reading, reading location, and further business relevant data are logged as events and stored in dedicated IT systems of supply chain parties in a distributed manner.

Event data can be employed for a number of purposes, e.g., to verify certain goods or to identify the location of products affected by product recalls. In particular, with the help of gathered event data, heuristics can be used to validate the authenticity of products within seconds when passing them from one supply chain participant to the next. Furthermore, they can provide advices for decision taking when dealing with unknown suppliers or substitution products.

The transformation toward an RFID-aided supply chain requires new technical equipment for capturing events and IT systems to store and exchange event data with other supply chain participants. Supply chain participants need to face the automatic exchange of event data with business partners for the very first time. Data protection of sensitive business secrets is therefore the major aspect that needs to be clarified before companies will start to adopt required transformation steps. The given work contributes toward data protection in EPCglobal networks as follows:

- Design of transparent security extensions for EPCglobal networks for device and business-level software,
- Definition of authentication protocols for devices with low computational resources, e.g., RFID tags,
- Development of an access control mechanism for software components in EPCglobal networks based on the analysis of the complete query history to automatically protect event data,
- Design of a fine-grained continuous filtering of event data instead of a currently widely used binary access decision,
- Implementation of history-based access control based on an in-memory database to enable a real-time analysis of the complete query history, and
- Integration of security extensions into the FOSSTRAK architecture to evaluate their applicability in context of the pharmaceutical industry.

The security extensions focus on event data since they need to be considered as sensitive data. Their knowledge can be misused to derive business secrets, e.g., business relationships. The given work defines strict requirements for the response time behavior of the security extensions to preserve a competitive advantage for business processes, e.g., during product receipt.

References

European Commission. Report on EU Customs Enforcement of IP Rights, (2009) http://ec.europa.eu/taxation_customs/resources/documents/customs/customs_controls/counterfeit_piracy/statistics/2009_statistics_for_2008_full_report_en.pdf1. Accessed 8 Mar 2012

H. Forcinio, *White Paper: The Business Value of RFID* (Microsoft Corporation, WA, 2006)

Chapter 1
Introduction

The given work addresses an organizational and a technical issue. Both are considered individually throughout my dissertation.

Organizational Context: From an organizational perspective, current businesses are confronted with continuously challenging factors, such as changing business partners and interchangeable products, when dealing with new business partners. On the one hand, building on a static supply chain helps reducing these factors since supplier and customer know each other and have proofed to be reliable partners for years. On the other hand, static supply chains result in limiting factors, such as performing business with a limited set of partners. In a globalized market, supply chains tend to transform to increasingly dynamic and open supply networks that build on mutual exchange of products with new and even unknown business partners. As a result, more and more suppliers compete for the lowest price, i.e. consumers can easily switch between various vendors of standardized goods.

I refer to *EPCglobal Networks* as supply chain networks that associate a digital representation to all handled physical goods. Product meta data are stored in a distributed manner in individual event repositories of all involved supply chain parties. The existence of digital product meta data supports business processes, such as tracking and tracing of products, exchanging advice letters, goods receipt, etc. EPCglobal networks aim to involve the goods' meta data in existing business processes, e.g. to verify product's authenticity automatically during goods receipt. However, exchanging meta data automatically results in certain security risks, e.g. competitors or attackers can derive business secrets. Security threats are discussed in Sect. 3.1.

This work addresses the problem of protecting sensitive business secrets while exposing goods' meta data for certain supply chain parties and business cases in an automatic way. The main contribution is the introduction of transparent security extensions for existing EPCglobal on device- and business-level to protect business secrets from being exposed to attackers or competitors.

Technical Context: From the technical perspective, my developed security extensions perform real-time analysis of the complete query history. Traditional

Matthieu-P. Schapranow, *Real-time Security Extensions for EPCglobal Networks*,
In-Memory Data Management Research, DOI: 10.1007/978-3-642-36343-6_1,
© Springer-Verlag Berlin Heidelberg 2014

access control mechanisms build on a bivalent decision taking, i.e. results of the set {*"declined"*, *"granted"*}. In contrast to them, the developed History-based Access Control (HBAC) enables a continuous spectrum of control from the interval [*"declined"*, *"granted"*]. Thus, it supports a more fine-grained way of data protection in contrast to existing access control techniques.

For example, if an inquirer is not allowed to access a certain subset of attributes of an EPC result set, the response is filtered. The filtering process is part of HBAC when enforcing inquirer-specific access rights.

Traditional access control mechanisms involve the definition and assignment of proper access rights to all involved parties before granting access to certain resources. In contrast, my developed security extensions support access rules that protect business secrets without assigning individual rights. In addition, the given contribution involves analysis of the complete query history when taking an access decision. This requires the following challenges to be addressed: (a) storage requirements of the continuously increasing query history, (b) real-time analysis of the history, and (c) adaptation of predefined access rights based on the results of the analysis of the query history. Depending on the history and access rules specific access decisions are taken.

1.1 Challenges in Pharmaceutical Supply Chains

The European pharmaceutical industry hit headlines with operation MEDI-FAKE announcing 34 million confiscated fake drugs in just two months [1]. The European Commission (EC) reported an increase of 118 % for pharmaceutical counterfeits detected at borders in 2008 compared to 2007. The pharmaceutical product category is the third largest product category in terms of quantities of intercepted articles in addition to the categories CDs/DVDs and tobacco [2]. Recent research results focusing on the ingredients of anti-malarial products from eleven African countries indicated these products contained either a low portion or none of the active ingredient Artemisinin [3]. Counterfeited drugs are a risk for customers and suppliers, since their effects are neither tested nor validated and the customer may suffer from medical complications. Approx. 7,000 annual cases of medical complications in the U.S. are linked to pharmaceutical counterfeits or the use of improper ingredients [4]. For example, FDA warned about the risk of using unapproved injectable anti-cancer products in early 2012 [5]. Moreover, concrete counterfeits of the anti-cancer medicine Avastin were identified in the U.S. in February 2012 [6].

In 2004, it was estimated that more than 500 billion USD were traded in counterfeits, i.e. 7 % of the world trade in the same period [7]. It is argued, that this equals an increase of 150 billion USD compared to 2001 [8]. During the same period, the worldwide merchandise trade increased only by approx. 50 billion USD.

This brief excerpt of reported cases and their impact highlights the omnipresent risks of counterfeits and the need for a reliable mechanism to protect products.

This protection has to be an integer part of the entire supply chain and should involve all supply chain participants. A high level of supply chain integrity is the basis for reliable product tracking and counterfeit detection.

The European pharmaceutical supply chain consists of more than 192,000 parties [9]. The availability of generic drugs transformed the pharmaceutical market towards a more open supply chain. For example, new pharmaceuticals for the German market must be licensed to obtain a "Pharmazentralnummer (PZN)" (central pharmaceutical number). The PZN is a relatively small restriction of admission. Once the manufacturer paid the fee for the usage of the PZN it can be used for a limited period of time without further investigations. The EC is working on an EU-wide standardization for unique identifiers and verification methods of medical products [10]. It proposes the integration of essential product details into the identifier, such as the manufacturer product code and package identifier. However, the current identification approaches lack the ability to identify pharmaceuticals on item level instead of batch level.

RFID technology enables gathering of location-based information of tagged items without establishing a direct line of sight. I am convinced it is a possible basis for protecting pharmaceutical goods [11]. All supply chain parties store event data in local Electronic Product Code Information Services (EPCIS) repositories that can be queried by other supply chain parties to retrieve details associated with products. I consider EPCIS repositories as standardized software products that store and manage access to event data, e.g. open source platform FOSSTRAK [12].

The adoption towards EPCglobal networks incorporates the facts: native cooperation of all supply chain parties, amortization of initial investments, and secured exchange of event data to improve existing business processes, e.g. goods receipt and anti-counterfeiting. EPCglobal networks build the basis for an integer supply chain by supervising movements of ingredients from suppliers to manufacturers and movements of products from manufacturers via intermediate supply chain parties to end consumers.

In Europe, approx. 30 billion pharmaceutical product units are manufactured annually of which approx. 50 % are only available on-prescription [9]. In the following, I focus on pharmaceuticals on-prescription base. Counterfeits of on-prescription medicines are more likely due to their higher retail price and customers that want to access them without having a valid prescription [13, Sect. 3.3.4]. Furthermore, I expect false composition of ingredients to harm or even to kill human beings, e.g. when an expected medical reaction is prevented or adverse effects occur.

Approx. 2,200 pharmaceutical manufacturers produce pharmaceutical goods that are shipped to 50,000 wholesalers within the EU. The latter deliver products in repacked transportation units to retailers (approx. 140,000 individuals) and finally to the consumer [9, 14]. In terms of the pharmaceutical supply chain, I consider the consumer as the sink of a product, e.g. a patient buying products in a pharmacy or a hospital. Only licensed retailers are permitted to sell on-prescription medicines in Europe, e.g. pharmacies, hospitals, etc. Between individual supply chain participants logistics provider are responsible for handling items and transferring

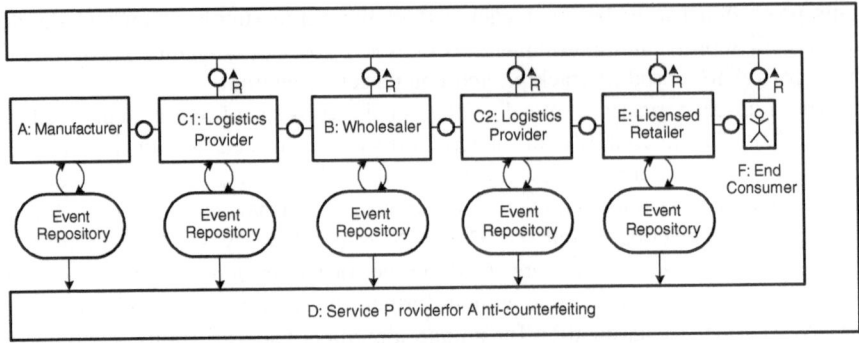

Fig. 1.1 Combined data and product flow between supply chain party roles *A..F* of an RFID-aided pharmaceutical supply chain. Service provider *D* accesses distributed EPCIS repositories of individual parties for verification of product authenticity

them. During goods receipt and goods shipment individual tracking events are recorded at the site of the handling supply chain party. Tracking goods is the basis for creating the virtual product history of a certain item, i.e. the item's path through the supply chain. A dedicated service provider, who is granted access to the EPCIS repositories of all supply chain parties, is required to reconstruct the item's history. The service provider is the basis for validating the authenticity of the pharmaceuticals and to detect counterfeits based on consistency checks of data gathered from distributed EPCIS repositories. Figure 1.1 shows the interaction of EPCIS repositories of individual supply chain parities and the service provider modeled using the Fundamental Modeling Concepts (FMC) [15]. In the remainder of my work, I assume the absence of the inference concept for EPCglobal networks. *Inference* describes an approach to reduce event data by scanning boxes and pallets instead of their individual contents, i.e. the path of a concrete product needs to be reconstructed beyond boxing and unboxing operations [16, Chap. 31]. That means, content of packaging units, such as boxes, pallets, containers is not inferred from its containment relationship by evaluating add and delete events occurred at various stages within the supply chain. I consider this as a task of the Electronic Product Code Discovery Services, which is not investigated in further detail in the context of my work.

The service provider is a trusted instance that can be queried by all supply chain participants. For example, customers can make use of an online web portal or public reader terminals in pharmacies. The implementation considerations for a dedicated service provider proposed by me forms the basis for further discussions [14].

EPCglobal networks can provide a possible infrastructure for reliable product tracking and tracing across the entire supply chain [11]. However, RFID technology—only one possible implementation for EPCglobal networks—was not designed for secured data exchange of confidential details. Hence, a variety of new data security threats arise when migrating towards an RFID-aided supply chain. Security requirements for RFID environments are investigated in further details in Chap. 3.

On the one hand, I consider the usage of EPCglobal networks as a major improvement for involved business processes by providing fine-grained data about handled goods. It supports identification of ingredients from suppliers to manufacturers and products from manufacturers to customers. For example, EPCglobal networks support tracking of individual products and help to distinguish them from mass products. Furthermore, their individual paths from suppliers via all involved supply chain parties are documented. On the other hand, I stress that data exchanged via EPCglobal networks can be misused to derive business internals, e.g. supplier relationships, product ingredients, and customer relationships. Qualified attacks against EPCglobal components and systematic combination of responses returned by EPCIS repositories form the basis for knowledge extraction by competitors. The given dissertation aims to control access to sensitive business data while incorporating EPCglobal components for automatic data exchange.

1.2 Problem Statement and Hypotheses

In the following, I introduce my selected problem statement and corresponding hypotheses. The latter draw the motivation of my work since I am going to prove or disprove their correctness with the help of the given contributions.

The integrity of existing supply chains is a fragile construct. When migrating to EPCglobal networks, new fine-grained data are shared between supply chain parties. On the one hand, this enables precise control of fast moving goods, e.g. to establish industry-wide anti-counterfeiting [17]. On the other hand, the exposure of these data can be misused to derive sensitive business secrets or to inject counterfeited products into the market [18].

Event Data: In the remainder of my work, I refer to *events* in context of EPC-global networks as tuples, which consist at least of the following attributes [19, Sect. 7.2.8]:

- **Unique Product Identifiers:** A list of unique identifiers of products the event is associated with, e.g. the individual Electronic Product Code (EPC),
- **Event Time:** The timestamp when the event occurred,
- **Record Time:** The timestamp when the event was recorded,
- **Action:** With respect to the lifecycle of the EPC, the involved action when the event occurred, e.g. ADD, OBSERVE, or DELETE, and
- **Read Point:** The location, where the event occurred.

In contrast to the EPCglobal definition, I consider the read point as mandatory detail, e.g. for business processes to locate the concrete product. Events may also contain further optional details, such as involved business steps, business locations, and sensor data of active tags. EPCglobal defines the following core events types: object, aggregation, quantity, and transaction [19, Sect. 7.2].

Listing A.5 in Appendix A.4 shows event data serialized within a SOAP response body. Lines 5–14 show an event for action OBSERVE. It consists of the serialized unique product identifier urn:epic:id:sgtin:1301757845.008.000133753170, the event timestamp 00:11 a.m. at Oct. 4, 2010, and the serialized read point urn:epic:id:sgln:1301757845.66446365.2. Furthermore, it contains details about business step, business location, and record time. Event data build the foundation of EPCglobal networks. They enable fine-grained tracking and tracing of products, e.g. for anti-counterfeiting. EPCglobal networks require the automatic exchange of event data via EPCIS. However, unauthorized access to event data or their unsecured exchange result in data leakage, exposure of confidential business secrets, relationships, or product ingredients. For further details about concrete security threats in EPCglobal networks, please refer to Sect. 3.1.

Liability: EPCglobal networks build the foundation of improved business processes, such as anti-counterfeiting, verification of product authenticity, and detection of counterfeit injection. I focus on the benefits of EPCglobal networks with respect to anti-counterfeiting in my work. For example, the liability for improper effects of counterfeited pharmaceuticals is widely discussed. The manufacturer of the original product is currently considered as the party that is reliable for side effects of counterfeited product unless the customer can clearly distinguish between authentic and counterfeited products [20]. Faked pharmaceuticals may harm or even kill human beings.

EPCglobal networks are motivated by anti-counterfeiting techniques based on the analysis of event data and the need for supply chains integrity. Unless event data are considered as sensitive and still exchanged in clear text without any protection against manipulation or eavesdropping, it remains questionable whether they build a reliable basis for anti-counterfeiting. My research activities are driven by the idea that real-time security extensions throughout the supply chain can be used to restrict the injection of counterfeited goods into supply chains by automatically analyzing the product's meta data.

The title of my work points to a dedicated real-time aspect. It stresses the fact that access to event data needs to be granted or declined within milliseconds to prevent blocking of existing business processes that depend on the outcome of the access decision. I refer to *real-time* as the access decision of the security extensions taken within an empiric time frame of less than two seconds as stated in Hyp. 1. I consider EPCglobal networks as a possible basis for anti-counterfeiting, which support the reconstruction of time and location of a possible counterfeit injection. As a result, the stated liability problem can be shifted to the supply chain party that accepted an untested product after counterfeit injection.

Problem Statement: Is it possible to establish new business relationships in open supply chain and to automatically exchange event data while protecting business secrets?

Nowadays, manufacturers control their suppliers and customers in closed supply chains, e.g. in the automotive industry. As a result, manufacturers are able to verify suppliers' products before deciding to use products of a new supplier. In addition, manufacturers define product characteristics that need to be fulfilled by the supplier, e.g. time to deliver, packaging size, details contained in the advice letter, etc.

Open supply chains present the challenge of how to initially trust unknown or new supply chain parties, e.g. new suppliers. I define the problem of how to initiate a new relationship between business partners within open supply chains as an initial trust problem. In the remainder of the work, I refer to *trust* as the absence of complete certainty. Since defining and measuring trust is not the focus of this work, I consider this brief definition as feasible to motivate the initial trust problem. Furthermore, unknown wholesalers or customers result in the risk of business infiltration, e.g. competitors that try to obtain details about suppliers, product ingredient or involved third parties [18]. I consider business secrets as sensitive, which are protected by design in closed supply chains.

Supply chains are more and more optimized to improve Key Performance Indicators (KPIs), such as on stock availability, transportation costs, and on-time delivery [21]. Nowadays, one of major competitive KPIs is conformance to promised delivery time. As a result, the electronic exchange of product meta data, e.g. delivery date or advice letter, is performed before its physical pendant is delivered. Combining the advantages of automatic exchange of product meta data, e.g. through EPCglobal networks, with open supply chains, results in new challenges for IT systems of involved supply chain partners.

Hypotheses: In my dissertation, I define alternatives to protect sensitive business secrets while enabling automatic exchange of product meta data in EPCglobal networks. Furthermore, my approach supports the use of implicit access rules that are evaluated with the help of the complete query history to control access to data that might expose business secrets when semantically combined. It further supports explicit definition of access rights for individual supply chain partners and groups and to enable a fine-grained access control. My contribution introduces access control for EPCglobal networks that are currently out of scope of EPCglobal specifications.

Granularity of Protection of Fine-Grained Event Data
Data stored in event repositories can vary in quantity and level of detail. Depending on the business relation with the querying party, the amount of data and the degree of detail that is shared needs to be controlled to confirm with the principle of data minimalism [22, 23].

Hypothesis 1 Validation and adaption of access rights based on the analysis of the complete query history can be performed in real-time during query processing, i.e. in less than two seconds.

Prevention of Anonymous Attacks against EPCglobal Information Systems
EPCglobal networks require open interfaces that can be queried for details about handled goods [24, Sect. 9]. It raises the question how to prevent anonymous

attacks by counterfeiters or competitors against these interfaces to obtain event data or to derive sensitive business secrets.

Hypothesis 2 Public Key Infrastructure (PKI) certificates for identification of supply chain parties can be used to establish specific access control and to trace counterfeiters or attackers once they were detected.

Exposure of Encryption Keys
Encryption is an established way to securely exchange sensitive data. However, once the encryption key is exposed, the encrypted content is no longer secured.

Hypothesis 3 Management of individual encryption keys per supply chain participant can reduce impact of key exposure. Thus, in case of disaster, malicious clients can be blocked individually without affecting other supply chain participants. Using an in-memory database supports multiple key renewals per day and individual key lookups in an interactive manner.

1.3 Research Methods and Structure of the Work

The given work represents the results of my research activities. I followed a *system engineering* approach for IT systems in the course of my work. For better understanding, I introduce a common understanding of system engineering in context of IT systems.

Sommerville defines system engineering as being "[...] concerned with all aspects of computer-based systems development, including hardware, software and process engineering" [25, Sect. 1.1]. He understands software engineering as a specific part of the system engineering process. Laplante defines software engineering as a "[...] systematic approach to the analysis, design, assessment, implementation, test, maintenance and reengineering of software, that is, the application of engineering to software" [26]. Boehm states that software engineering is the "[...] application of science and mathematics by which the properties of software are made useful to people. [It] includes computer science and the sciences of making things useful to people: Behavioral sciences, economics, management sciences" [27].

This is only a small choice of existing definitions for system and software engineering, but they already show how difficult it is to precisely define the term system engineering. Therefore, I provide my personal definition for system engineering in context of scientific work as follows.

My dissertation follows a system engineering approach to identify and evaluate related scientific work, understand and analyze existing software systems, define requirements to design functionality, and to implement structures with the aim to improve and secure certain aspects of daily life.

This definition provides the framework for my work. It contains a four-folded understanding of the term system engineering as follows:

- Analysis and evaluation of existing work,
- Definition of requirements,
- Design and implementation, and
- Measurement of improvements for daily life.

In addition, I followed the design science methodology [28]. With reference to the latter, I developed and evaluated a concrete IT artifact—security extensions for EPCglobal networks—to address organizational requirements—in practice: to protect business secrets in open supply chains based on EPCglobal networks. The business perspective is driven by the need for protection of sensitive business data while having a competitive advantage in goods processing. From the technical perspective, EPCglobal networks come with threats to derive sensitive business data not publicly available today.

Structure of the Work: The rest of the given work is structured as follows. The work is motivated by presenting a case study of the pharmaceutical industry in Europe in Chap. 1. Due to the possible impact on the health constitution of human beings receiving medicines, counterfeits of pharmaceuticals are chosen to connect the scientific work with its practical relevance. In Chap. 2 components of current EPCglobal networks and the scope of my current work in context of related work are presented. Dedicated security requirements for these components are defined in Chap. 3. Security extensions for device-level and business-level are discussed in Chaps. 4 and 5 respectively. The latter builds the primary focus of the given work. As a result, business-level security extensions are applied to an existing event repository. In Chap. 6 the introduced security extensions are discussed in context

Table 1.1 Mapping of design science aspects to corresponding chapters

Design science aspect	Description
Problem relevance	In Chap. 1 the organizational context and the problem statement are defined, which consider the business and the technology perspective
Research rigor	I followed a structured IT systems engineering approach, a mapping of system engineering and thesis structure is given in Table 1.2
Design as a search process	The developed security extensions are a result of an iterative development process integrating feedback from scientific and business audiences
Design as an artifact	In Chaps. 4 and 5 artifacts of my research activities for business and technical requirements are presented
Design evaluation	Chapter 7 conducts an evaluation of my dissertation considering business and technical aspects
Research contributions	In addition to the designed artifacts qualitative and quantitative aspects of my research results are discussed in Chap. 6
Research communication	My research results were presented to technical and business interested audience to receive feedback about feasibility and applicability of the presented research artifacts. Selected publications are referenced throughout the dissertation

Table 1.2 Mapping of software engineering aspects to corresponding chapters

Software engineering aspect	Corresponding chapter
Analysis	Chap. 2
Definition	Chap. 3
Design and implementation	Chaps. 4 and 5
Measurement	Chap. 6

of the case study and in Chap. 7 their applicability to further industries and problems is evaluated. The given work concludes with a summary in Chap. 8.

I consider the combination of technical and business requirements as the extremes that engineering needs to address. Thus, the given dissertation combines both aspects for the given problem statement. The outline of my work combines business and technical requirements and corresponding design decisions. For convenient navigation within this document, I prepared mappings from design science and engineering aspects to corresponding chapters and sections. Table 1.1 gives an overview of design science aspects and their location within my work. Engineering aspects and their mapping to corresponding sections within the given work are provided in Table 1.2.

References

1. IP Crime Group, IP Crime Report, (2008)
2. European Commission, Report on EU Customs Enforcement of IP Rights (2009), http://ec.europa.eu/taxation_customs/resources/documents/customs/customs_controls/counterfeit_piracy/statistics/2009_statistics_for_2008_full_report_en.pdf. Accessed 8 Mar 2012
3. P.N. Newton et al., Poor quality vital anti-malarials in Africa—an urgent neglected public health priority. Malaria J. **10**(1), 352 (2011)
4. J. Jenkins, P. Mills, R. Maidment, M. Profit, Pharma Traceability Bus. Case Rep. (2007)
5. Food and Drug Administration, FDA notifies health care providers about the risks of purchasing unapproved injectable cancer medications from unlicensed source (2012), http://www.fda.gov/downloads/Drugs/DrugSafety/DrugIntegrityandSupplyChainSecurity/UCM287717.pdf. Accessed 8 Mar 2012
6. Food and Drug Administration. Unapproved Versions of Injectable Cancer Medications Could Result in Serious Harm to Your Patients; One Counterfeit Version Found (2012), http://www.fda.gov/downloads/Drugs/DrugSafety/DrugIntegrityandSupplyChainSecurity/UCM287717.pdf. Accessed 8 Mar 2012
7. ICC Policy Statement. The Fight against Piracy and Counterfeiting of Intellectual Property (2003), http://www.iccwbo.org/home/intellectual_property/fight_against_piracy.pdf. Accessed 8 Mar 2012
8. T. Staake, F. Thiesse, E. Fleisch, Extending the EPC network: the potential of RFID in anti-counterfeiting, in *Proceedings of the ACM Symposium on Applied Computing* (ACM, New York, 2005) pp. 1607–1612
9. J. Müller et al., A simulation of the pharmaceutical supply chain to provide realistic test data, in *Proceedings of 1st International Conference on Advances in System Simulation.* IEEE, (2009)

10. European Commission, Delegated Act on the Detailed Rules for a Unique Identifier for Medical Products for Human Use and its Verification (2011), http://ec.europa.eu/health/files/counterf_par_trade/safety_2011-11.pdf. Accessed 8 Mar 2012
11. Bundesverband Informationswirtschaft, Telekommunikation und neue Medien. White Paper RFID Technologie, Systeme und Anwendungen (2005), http://www.bitkom.org/files/documents/White_Paper_RFID_deutsch_11.08.2005__final.pdf. Accessed 8 Mar 2012
12. Fosstrak, Project License (2009), http://www.fosstrak.org/epcis/license.html. Accessed 8 Mar 2012
13. IMPACT Secretariat at AIFA, The handbook, in *Proceedings of the International Medical Products Anti-Counterfeiting, 2011, Taskforce* ed. by IMPACT. Accessed 8 Mar 2012
14. M-P. Schapranow, J. Müller, A. Zeier, H. Plattner, RFID event data processing: an architecture for storing and searching, in *Proceedings of the 4th International Workshop on RFID Technology—Concepts, Applications, Challenges* 2010
15. A. Knöpfel, B. Gröne, P. Tabeling, *Fundamental Modeling Concepts Effective Communication of IT Systems*, (John, Hoboken, 2005)
16. M. Davison, *Pharmaceutical Anti-Counterfeiting: Combating the Real Danger from Fake Drugs*. (John, Hoboken, 2011)
17. M-P. Schapranow et al., *What are Authentic Pharmaceuticals Worth?* Chapter 13, (INTECH Press, 2011), pp. 203–220
18. M-P. Schapranow, M. Lorenz, A. Zeier, Ha. Plattner, License-based Access Control in EPCglobal Networks, in *Proceedings of 7th European Workshop on Smart Objects: Systems, Technologies and Applications*. VDE, 2011
19. Global Standards 1. EPCIS Standard 1.0.1 (2007), http://www.gs1.org/gsmp/kc/epcglobal/epcis/epcis_1_0_1-standard-20070921.pdf. Accessed 8 Mar 2012
20. C.C. Blance, Pharmaceutical counterfeiting: the effect of technology, regulation, and legislation on manufacturer liability. Mass Torts. **8**(2), (2010)
21. F.G, Knolmayer, P. Mertens, A. Zeier, *Supply Chain Management Based on SAP Systems: Architecture and Planning Processes SAP Excellence* (Springer, London, 2009)
22. Federal Office for Information Security, BSI Standard 100–1: Information Security Management, System V. 1.5, (2008)
23. M-P. Schapranow, A. Zeier, H. Plattner, Security extensions for improving data security of event repositories in EPCglobal networks, in *Proceedings of the 9th International Conference on Ubiquitous, Computing* 2011
24. Global Standards 1. The EPCglobal Architecture Framework 1.4 (2010), http://www.gs1.org/gsmp/kc/epcglobal/architecture/architecture_1_4-framework-20101215.pdf. Accessed 8 Mar 2012
25. I. Sommerville, *Software Engineering* (Addison-Wesley, Boston, 2007)
26. Phillip A. Laplante, *What Every Engineer Should Know about Software Engineering*. (Taylor & Francis, New York, 2007)
27. B. Boehm, A View of 20th and 21st Century Software Engineering: ICSE 2006 Keynote Address (2006)
28. A.R. Hevner, S.T. March, J. Park, S. Ram, Design science in information systems research. MIS Q. **28**(1), 75–105 (2004)

Chapter 2
Related Work

The following chapter presents findings on selected related work and places my work in the corresponding context. There are two categories of related work with relevance to my work that are considered in this chapter:

- Related work dealing with access control, which is a special mechanism to expose data to authorized parties only, is presented in Sect. 2.1, and
- Related work dealing with EPCglobal networks and securing its components is presented in Sect. 2.2.

The first category is considered to outline existing techniques for protection of sensitive data, their limitations, and their applicability with respect to EPCglobal networks. The second is considered to present and evaluate standards introduced by the EPCglobal consortium, derive trends of ongoing security activities in this context, and to introduce the technical foundations of EPCglobal networks. In Sect. 2.3 the analysis results of related work are classified.

2.1 Access Control Mechanisms

Security aspects are typically researched to address a certain threat, platform, software, use case, etc. In the following, I place my work in context of related work on access control systems.

I define *access control* as all efforts to limit various actions $a \in A$ to sensitive resources $r \in R$ to a certain user $u \in U$. Access control can formally be defined as a triplet as given in Eq. 2.1. In context of EPCglobal networks, I focus on event data as the resources that need to be protected, i.e. $R = \{\text{EPC events}\}$.

$$(a, r, u) \forall a \in A, r \in R, u \in U \qquad (2.1)$$

Discretionary Access Control (DAC) describes a class of mechanisms that controls access by leaving the access decision to the user [1]. In other words, once a certain user is granted access to a resource, she/he is able to grant access for a certain

Matthieu-P. Schapranow, *Real-time Security Extensions for EPCglobal Networks*,
In-Memory Data Management Research, DOI: 10.1007/978-3-642-36343-6_2,
© Springer-Verlag Berlin Heidelberg 2014

resource to further users. Even if there is only limited access defined for a certain resource, e.g. read-only, the user is able to create a copy of the resource's content and grant individual access for further users to the copied content, which results in data exposure. For example, representatives of DAC are Access Control Lists (ACLs) incorporated by the operating system Microsoft Windows and owner-group-other flags of Unix for controlling access to files. The counterpart of DAC is referred to as Non-Discretionary Access Control (NDAC), i.e. access is not directly controlled by the user, but by a dedicated administrative entity [1].

Role-Based Access Control: Role-based Access Control (RBAC) defines a superclass for access control mechanisms that enforce access rights and restrictions on working roles rather than on individuals [2]. RBAC decouples user management from access management. To do so, RBAC controls access to resources by controlling actions A performed by users U on resources R.

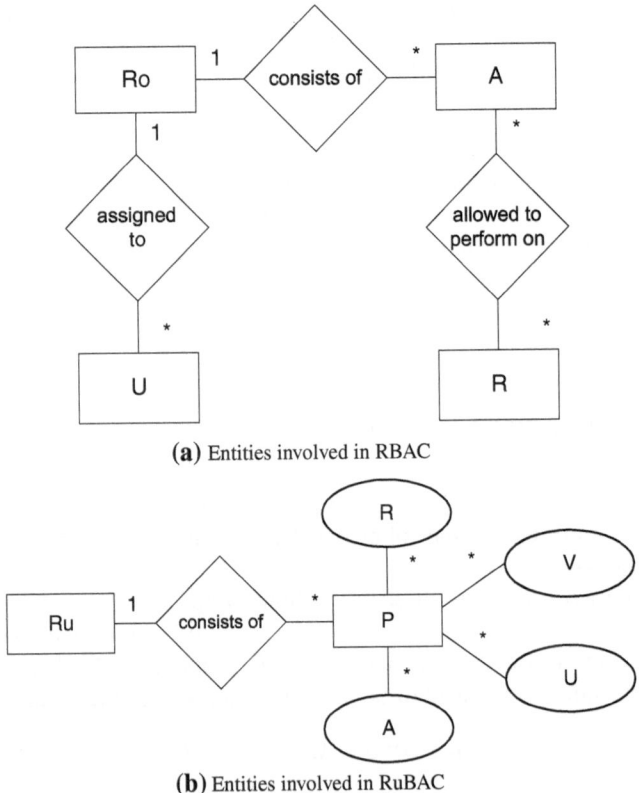

(**a**) Entities involved in RBAC

(**b**) Entities involved in RuBAC

Fig. 2.1 Comparison of access control mechanisms using entity relationship diagrams: (**a**) RBAC controls allowed actions on resources via roles while (**b**) RuBAC controls access via rules evaluating predicates (*A* actions, *P* predicates, *R* resources, *Ro* roles, *Ru* rules, *U* users, *V* additional decision data)

In contrast to traditional access control, RBAC groups allowed actions A in roles Ro as depicted in Fig. 2.1a. There is no direct mapping between resources R and users U due to the indirection introduced by the roles concept. Formally, RBAC can be understood as set of tuples with $A_{ro} = (\{a \in A|$ permitted by $ro\}, R_{ro} = \{r \in R|ro$ is granted access to $\})$ and $U_{ro} = (\{u \in U|$ assigned to $ro\})$ as defined in Eq. 2.2.

$$RBAC = \{(A_{ro}, R_{ro}) \times U_{ro}\}, ro \in Ro \qquad (2.2)$$

With the assumption that the number of users is larger than the number of active roles, RBAC results in reduced maintainability. For example, granting access to the location attribute of gathered event data to all colleagues working as packers becomes a single task. Rather than identifying all packers within the company and setting their individual access rights, all colleagues working as role `Packer` are assigned with the right to read EPC event location. Thus, all packers get immediate access to the required event data in a transparent way. Furthermore, also newly joined colleagues are automatically granted the access rights to read EPC event location. However, this results in the disadvantage, that people's role membership has to be supervised otherwise access rights might be expanded while certain persons are no longer allowed to get access. For instance, if there are two mutually excluding roles defined to establish a Separation of Duties (SoD) and a certain person is assigned to both roles, SoD is violated although RBAC is applied [1].

Nevertheless, I value RBAC as a concept that improves handling of access for a potentially infinite number of users. In terms of the pharmaceutical supply chain as described in Sect. 1.1 the number of users of a certain EPCIS repository is not known beforehand. In contrast to the number of involved goods and parties in the pharmaceutical supply chain, I expect the amount of active roles to be comparable small. Firstly, it is reasonable to distinguish between direct partners, who receive goods without involved third parties, and indirect partners, which receive goods via further intermediates roles in accordance with their place in the supply chain role. Secondly, roles can be used to group goods in categories and control access via this indirection. Thirdly, special classifications introduced by the supply chain party can be used to value certain partners, e.g. high and low priority business partners or suppliers.

This example shows two aspects of RBAC. Firstly, roles cannot be predefined due to the variety of possible classification criteria. Secondly, grouping individual inquirers into roles helps to abstract from the unknown number of inquirers and keeps access control as a limited task rather than as a regular task when an unknown inquirer is querying.

In context of EPCglobal networks and the given pharmaceutical scenario, RBAC supports abstraction of individuals. As a result, the administrative overhead for maintaining possibly hundred of thousands individual access rights vanishes. Thus, I consider RBAC as one way to reduce the complexity. In the given dissertation, RBAC is applied to definition and enforcement of access rights as described in Sect. 5.2.

Rule-Based Access Control: Rule-based Access Control (RuBAC) refers to all access control mechanisms defining access rights or restriction in a set of rules that need to be evaluated for each access request [1]. In other words, "RuBAC is a general term for access control systems that allows some form of organization-defined rules" [3]. RuBAC results in the advantage of defining various kinds of complex rules based on any kind of additional attributes, such as remote host name, current time, user details, etc. As a result, RuBAC enables a more fine-grained access control than RBAC. However, a concrete definition of rules and its interpretation needs to be implemented individually. RuBAC defines a set of rules Ru consisting of predicates P that are evaluated specifically when a concrete user u is accessing a certain resource r to perform an action a. Formally, RuBAC can be represented as given in Eq. 2.3 and depicted in Fig. 2.1b.

$$Ru = \{P(a, r, u, v)\})\forall a \in A, r \in R, u \in U, \{v \in V| \text{ decision data}\} \qquad (2.3)$$

RuBAC results in a higher flexibility when granting access. In the given dissertation, RuBAC is incorporated to adapt access rights accordingly to the history of granted access rights as described in Sect. 5.2.

The contributed HBAC combines RBAC and RuBAC to control access to event data in a holistic way as described in Sect. 5.1.

Extensible Access Control Markup Language: The eXtensible Access Control Markup Language (XACML) is an eXtensible Markup Language (XML) dialect specified by the OASIS consortium. It aims to define access control rights for subjects representing users, resources, and action based on rules and policies [4]. In addition, XACML introduces a conceptual SoD for access control systems, which is also applicable for the given work. Table 2.1 presents XACML duties, its brief description and a mapping to components of my work with direct references for further reading.

The use of XML for definition of access rights is a common approach as shown by the classification of related work. This standardized way of communication contributes to the interoperability between various software systems and vendors. In addition, it makes the automatic transformation of data formats possible, e.g. by using an eXtensible Stylesheet Language Transformations (XSLTs) [5]. However, in addition to XACML, which is only rarely used for RFID-specific developments, various extensions or other XML dialects are used, such as aidXACML or EAL introduced by Grummt et al. [6].

Open Digital Rights Language: The Open Digital Rights Language (ORDL) is a XML dialect for defining and maintaining rights of asset [7]. Assets in context of ODRL are mainly multimedia contents, such as audio or video contents. In the given work, I consider event data as company-specific assets comparable to purchased multimedia contents. Event data can be accessed by various inquirers but with individual access rights. Once a certain criterion has expired accessing event data must no longer be possible. I decided to make use of ODRL for definition of access rights and access control information for my contribution since it is a

Table 2.1 Mapping of XACML duties to sections within this document

XACML	Description	HBAC	Section
Policy Enforcement Point (PEP)	Component that enforces the decision issued by the PDP, i.e. interacting with the user and the resource to grant access to	Access Control Client (ACC)	5.1.3
Policy Decision Point (PDP)	Component that issues and revokes valid policies, e.g. based on external information, such as the querying user, history, context, etc.	Access Control Server (ACS)	5.1.4
Policy Administration Point (PAP)	Component responsible for managing policies, i.e. creating or modifying or access rights	Configuration Tool	5.1.5
Policy Information Point (PIP)	Component that provides additional information for the PDP to derive decisions	Trust Relationship Server (TRS)	5.1.6

lightweight approach and reduces data processing overhead. However, a homomorphism can be defined that transforms ODRL to the more expressive XACML, i.e. XACML is another possible implementation for definition of access rights.

2.2   Components of EPCglobal Networks

The EPCglobal consortium—newly also known as Global Standards 1 (GS1)—defines technical components and standards for intercommunication in RFID-aided supply chains. EPCglobal standards can be grouped in the functional layers identification, capturing, and exchanging as depicted in Fig. 2.2 [8].

The *identification* layer deals with the data format stored on tags, e.g. Tag Data Standard (TDS), and its translation, e.g. Tag Data Translation (TDT).

The *capturing* layer defines the communication protocol between tags and readers, e.g. Tag Protocol UHF Class 1 Gen1, EPC HF, and the Low Level Reader Protocol (LLRP), which is responsible for data acquisition and event capturing. On top, the Discovery Configuration and Initialization (DCI) and the Reader Management (RM) define how to discover and control distributed reader devices. The Application Level Events (ALE) standard defines how to handle, filter, and process reader events for software applications.

EPCIS bridge the gap between the layers *capture* and *exchange*. The Core Business Vocabulary (CBV) defines language elements used for data exchange. From the enterprise's point of view, the EPCIS provides high-level access methods for processing event data in enterprise applications, such as ERP systems. Object Name Service (ONS) and EPCDS perform lookup and discovery of resources, such as supply chain participants that handled a certain good. The standards

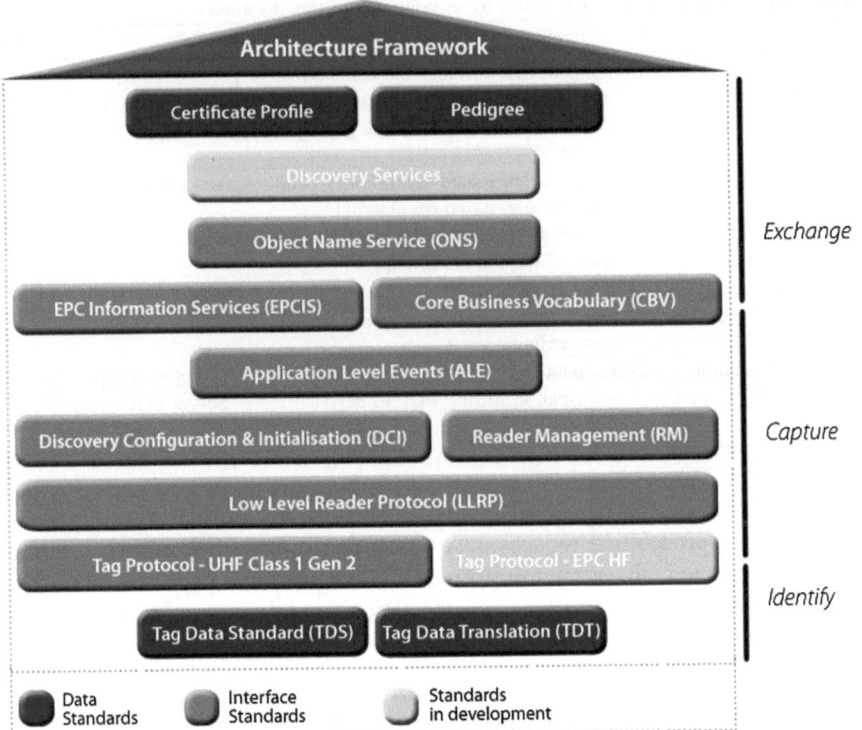

Fig. 2.2 Stack of EPCglobal standards taken from [8]. It consists of the layers tag identification, capture, and exchange of event data with business applications

Certificate Profile (CP) and Pedigree define data formats for exchanging data within EPCglobal networks from a business perspective.

I define EPCglobal networks as communication networks that exchange event data with the help of the components as defined by EPCglobal standards of the appropriate layer. In other words, EPCglobal networks contain only relevant components for business transactions, i.e. EPCglobal actors for EPCIS, ONS, and EPCDS. In addition to existing EPCglobal definition, I assume the existence of a generic service provider that performs business tasks not addressed by aforementioned components of EPCglobal networks, such as anti-counterfeiting.

RFID Tags
RFID tags consist of the components: (a) antenna, (b) integrated circuits, (c) data storage, and (d) optional equipment, such as sensors. They are tiny radio devices that can be distinguished according to (a) the operating frequency band, (b) the type of tag, and (c) their read-write capabilities.

Frequency Bands: The available radio band for RFID communication is defined by global standardization that can be restricted on a per-country basis [9].

Table 2.2 Classification of radio frequency bands used by RFID tags

Radio band	Frequency
Low Frequency (LF)	100–135 kHz
High Frequency (HF)	13.56 MHz
Ultra High Frequency (UHF)	868 MHz (Europe), 915 MHz (USA), 2.45 GHz (ISM)
Super High Frequency (SHF), Micro Wave (MW)	5.8 GHz

UHF tags are nowadays used for tracking and tracing scenarios due to the low power required for emitting signals

Table 2.2 gives an overview of available radio bands and their frequency in Europe and in the United States of America (USA). In comparison, current radio broadcasting based on FM operates in the frequency band 87.5–108 MHz, whereas former radio broadcasting was based on AM that operates in the frequency band Long Wave (LW) 148.5–283.5 kHz, Medium Wave (MW) 520–1,610 kHz, and Short Wave (SW) 2.3–26.1 MHz [10]. Furthermore, current cellular phones operate in the bands 900–1800 MHz (Europe), 850–1900 MHz (USA) respectively [11, Sect. 2.1]. Nowadays, UHF tags are mainly used for EPCglobal networks, i.e. their operating frequency is comparable to cellular phones or is located within the so-called Industrial, Scientific, and Medical (ISM) band.

Tag Types: The tag's type describes its capabilities. Keeping production costs low is a major requirement for passive RFID tags in EPCglobal networks for Near Field Communication (NFC) [12, Chap. 3]. Passive low-cost tags are powered by the physical principle of induction, i.e. they need to be placed near the reader's electromagnetic field, which is required for (a) power supply of the tag's integrated circuits and (b) data communication. In contrast to NFC, Far Field Communication (FFC) refers to communication when the distance between reader and tag exceeds one wavelength [13, Sect. 4.2.1.1]. FFC requires typically active RFID tags since they are able to actively modulate data via the radio band using their equipped battery. Table 2.3 compares the classification of tag capabilities.

Table 2.3 Classification of RFID tag types

Type	Functionality	Description
Passive	Induction	No power supply, powered by reader's electromagnetic induction, works only while in the reader's field
Semi-active	Induction, μC	Battery-powered, e.g. to perform regular sensor measurements, not for transmission
Active	Active transmission, μC	Battery-powered to extend transmission range and for regular sensor readings

Passive tags work only with an external stimulus. They are used due to their low manufacturing costs for nowadays tracking and tracing scenarios

Table 2.4 Read-write capabilities of RFID tags

Type	Description	Example
Read-only	Programmed once by the tag's manufacturer,	Toll systems, e.g. E-ZPass [14]
Write-once, Read-many	Programmed once by the product's manufacturer	Tags with EPCs [12]
Read-write	Content can be changed at any time	Cash card systems, e.g. PUCK [15]

Read-only tags are nowadays used for tracking and tracing scenarios due to the higher hardware requirements for read-write tags

Read-Write Capabilities: Read-write capabilities of RFID tags can be used to further classify tags. Three classes of tags exist according to their read-write capabilities: (a) read-only, (b) write-once, read-many, and (c) write-many, read-many tags [12, Chap. 7]. Table 2.4 gives a comparison of RFID tags based on its read-write capabilities. Read-only tags are a subset of Write-Once Read-Many (WORM) tags, but the tag's manufacturer initializes its content. The first user, e.g. the goods' manufacturer, initializes write-once, read-many tags. Write-many, read-many tags are equipped with a small flash storage comparable to external flash devices for personal computers that can be read and written multiple thousand times.

RFID Reader
RFID reader devices consist of (a) a set of antennas and (b) a controller device. The controller device implements radio interface protocols to communicate with RFID tags via the ether. Antennas are used to send out radio signals to tags and to receipt data.

Object Name Service
The ONS is a yellow page service for RFID-aided supply chains [16]. It returns for a given EPC the Unified Resource Locator (URL) of the manufacturer's EPCIS. The inquirer can contact the EPCIS of the manufacturer to obtain further details about the product and subsequent participants that handled a certain good identified by the EPC.

EPC Information Services
The EPCIS provides standardized interfaces between internal event repositories and external inquirers [17]. In other words, it is responsible for exchanging relevant internal data with external participants of the supply chain, e.g. to perform anti-counterfeiting. The EPCIS is also involved in controlling access to event data and to ensure privacy of internal data. Thus, I consider the EPCIS as a possible target of attackers to obtain event data.

EPC Discovery Services
The EPCDS acts as an intermediate for querying parties that pre-processes data from various EPCIS repositories and performs preliminary operations on them, e.g. aggregation of internal event data [18]. When the inference concept for supply

chains is applied, the EPCDS is required to reconstruct the virtual path of individual products. Up to now, there is no EPCDS implementation ratified by EPCglobal available since corresponding standards are still in development. However, Müller contributes with an EPCDS built on the in-memory building blocks as defined in Sect. 3.4 [19].

Middleware
The RFID middleware acts as a mediator between RFID readers and the capturing interface of the EPCIS repository. It fulfills a set of common tasks within a company to integrate event data in existing business systems, such as ERP systems. Furthermore, it is responsible for filtering and collecting events and for the harmonization of data format between EPCglobal components [17].

Security in EPCglobal Networks
The Certificate Profile (CP) is defined by the EPCglobal consortium and specifies security aspects in EPCglobal networks. The first version 1.0 was released in March 2006 and contains the sections "Introduction", "Algorithm Profile", "Certificate Profile", "Certificate Validation Profile", and two appendices, which are described in a total of 11 pages [20]. Latest released version 2.0 ratified in June 2010 consists of the identical outline in a total of 14 pages [21]. In the following, the content of the latest CP is summarized and evaluated.

The CP expects the use of X.509 certificates in context of EPCglobal networks, which requires a global PKI. From my perspective, this is feasible, since the use of PKIs has been proven to work for productive environments, such as device and user authentication 802.11x in communication networks and Germany's electronic identity cards [22, 23]. The rest of the CP provides recommendations about the use of X.509 certificates for identification purposes.

The section "Algorithm Profile" contains recommendations for X.509 certificates. As of today, it is recommended to use the following settings:

- Algorithm: sha2WithRSAEncryption, i.e. any of the algorithms SHA-224, SHA-256, SHA-384, SHA-512.
- Key length: 2,048 bits (3,072 bits by the year 2031).

The section "Certificate Profile" contains mainly a description on how to include an EPC's URI representation within a certificate and how to encode users, services, servers, readers and devices accordingly, e.g. by including their unique serial number and/or device specific Media Access Control (MAC) identifier [24].

Further details about how to ensure security aspects, such as authentication and how to use it in context of access control are not defined in the CP. Therefore, I evaluated the latest EPCIS standard version 1.0.1 ratified in September 2007 for definitions regarding security [17]. It contains a subsection dealing with authentication and one dealing with authorization. The former contains the indication that the EPCIS Query Control Interface can be used for authentication. In addition, a "non-normative explanation" is given, indicating that the use of mutual authentication is expected. Concrete implementations or definitions are missing. The section about authorization specifies the following actions as valid:

- Refuse a request completely by a generic `SecurityException`,
- Hide data, e.g. the list of business transactions, but remove entire event when hiding data results in misleading data,
- Return a subset of requested data only, e.g. only the first hundred matching events when querying all known events,
- Respond with coarser grained data than requested, e.g. substituting all company-internal locations, such as gate 1, assembly area 2, etc. by a common location for the company, and
- Limit the scope of a query to a certain client, e.g. to provide EPCIS repositories as Software-as-a-Service (SaaS) [25].

The business-level security extensions described in Chap. 5 incorporate the latter three aspects to restrict access of clients to event data. The CP contains further a "non-normative explanation" stating: "[...] the EPCIS specification does not take a position as to how authorization decisions are taken" [17]. I value my work as a concrete contribution to show how to handle these decisions and how to protect sensitive event data.

The term *security services* was recently mentioned in the context of EPCglobal standards. However, an actual definition or a draft is still missing during creation of this document. I consider the results of this work as a major step towards making security services for EPCglobal networks come true.

Official standards provide clues for incorporating security features and expect their usage. However, EPCglobal leaves detailed design decisions, implementation strategies, and concrete implementations are left open to the reader. These standards lack a comprehensive description of threats, attack scenarios, their impact on business processes and possible countermeasures. The transformation of a conventional supply chain towards an RFID-aided supply chain involves various security relevant adaptations, such as open interfaces for accessing EPCIS repositories [17]. Existing work shows various threats, their impact, and countermeasures. The given dissertation contributes in designing, developing, and implementing concrete security extensions for EPCglobal EPCIS repositories. The latter is considered as a possible target of attacks since it is the source of sensitive event data that can be misused by attackers to derive correlated business information [26].

2.3 Combination and Classification of Related Work

Historic Developments: The wish for data protection in information systems is as old as the existence of any kind of data. Historically speaking, during the early development of first computer systems in World War II, such as ENIAC, the aspect of data protection arose [27]. For instance, with the invention of radar systems airplane attacks could be detected by sending out a radio signal and observing its reflections [14]. Identification Friend or Foe (IFF) systems were developed to distinguish unknown aircrafts from each other. Friendly aircrafts were equipped with an IFF system that sent out a special signal in response to a detected radar signal [28]. Let us consider IFF systems as information systems since typical attacks for information system also apply for them. Further details about concrete threats for RFID-aided supply chains are described in Sect. 3.1. After introducing IFF systems, they were copied and security extensions, such as on-device encryption, were added to secure their operation [28].

Lampson defines "[...] all the mechanisms that control the access of a program to other things in the system" [29] as *protection*. This general definition contains the first indication of the nowadays more popular term *access control*. In his work, the primarily goal of adding protection to information systems is named as protecting users from their own or other users' malice. In context of my work, this is still valid, since the goal is to protect supply chain participants from malicious behavior—whether intended or unintended—of other supply chain participants, technical errors of other automatic information systems, competitors, counterfeiters, or any kind of attackers. In addition, Lampson discusses concepts of *access control matrices* as a strategy for protection. This concept is also incorporated by the given work. He names possible issues that reside in former hardware limitations of the year 1971. For instance, the complete access control matrix can grow fast depending on the amount of users and objects. Keeping it entirely in fast accessible main memory, is considered as a waste of resources since its capacity is limited and only single entries of the access control matrix need to be accessed at a certain moment [29].

In my work, I consider these hardware limitations as no longer valid. I keep the entire access control matrix in a compressed format in fast access main memory by incorporating in-memory technology as discussed in Sect. 3.4.

The historical examples show a common empiric paradigm that is still valid for modern information systems: aspects of data protection are rarely considered during the design phase. More often, data protection is investigated once a product is ready to sell and a critical number of users are running the system. After this critical mass has been reached, the product becomes a more attractive target for attackers. In context of EPCglobal networks, the EC has recognized this gap for RFID systems and released a recommendation on the implementation of privacy and data protection principles in applications supported by radio-frequency identification in 2009. It contains the explicit advice to overcome the gap of security by recommending that "[...] privacy and information security features should be built into RFID applications before their widespread use (principle of 'security and privacy-by-design')" [30]. In addition, it contains a list of guidelines and principles that should be considered while implementing RFID information systems to raise its acceptance.

Risk Assessment: From the risk assessment's point of view, classifications of security risks are helpful to identify threats, assess them, evaluate their monetary impact, and to design and implement countermeasures [31]. Garfinkel et al.

classify security risks accordingly to the location where they occur in one of the following classes [32]:

- **Inside the Supply Chain**: Locations and transportation systems controlled by supply chain participants,
- **Outside the Supply Chain**: Locations after the product left the control of supply chain partners and is operated by the customer, and
- **In the Transition Zone**: Locations when products are leaving from inside to outside the supply chain, e.g. when the product is handed to the customer.

The given work primarily addresses the security of event repositories and the involved data exchange. Thus, I address threats that belong to the categories inside the supply chain and within the transition zone.

Spiekermann performed neutral studies on the acceptance of RFID technology and Privacy Enhancing Technologies (PETs) in retail businesses. In her work, she comes to the result that "[...] consumers do value the service spectrum, which can be realized through RFID [but] they are willing to forgo these benefits in order to protect their privacy" [33]. As a result, I stress the fact that improving security by using transparent privacy protection mechanisms is mandatory to increase acceptance for RFID-aided supply chains.

In 2006, the National Institute of Standards and Technology (NIST) published a technical report assessing access control systems. It observes that a wide range of access control systems is based on XML-based policy languages, but all of them lack the capability to express historical-based policies [1, Sect. 3.6.3]. In context of EPCglobal networks the temporal and history aspect becomes more important since goods are moving from party to party and access rights need to be modified multiple times during the lifecycle of a certain product. During my research of related work for EPCglobal networks, I observed only a small amount of related works dealing with temporal access control [1, 34]. This has motivated me to focus on processing of the query history to contribute with an HBAC system based on in-memory data processing in the given work.

Classification: In the following, I classify related work corresponding to their categories: (a) related work dealing with access control management systems and (b) RFID-specific related work. Figure 2.3 depicts components of an RFID information system that might be addressed by RFID-specific work. Table 2.5 categorizes these components correspondingly to their physical location within the supply chain and their technology affinity. It shows that RFID tags and readers are systems embedded in hardware to perform frequent actions in a very fast response time. In contrast, the remaining components are software system components of the enterprise software architecture. As a result, different requirements for interoperability and standardization exist for both categories. The classification in internal and external components is the basis to identify security threats. Company internal components can be controlled by enterprise-wide security policies that are enforced by regular trainings or tests of personnel. In contrast, external components cannot be controlled by company policies. Therefore, external components

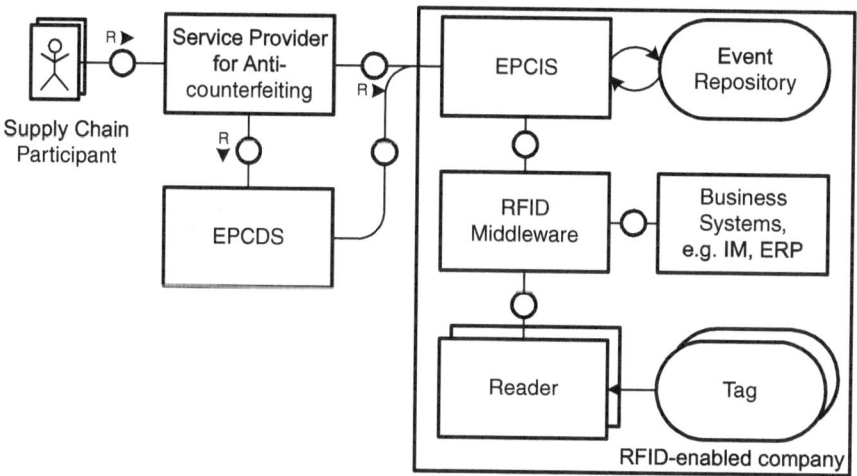

Fig. 2.3 Infrastructure components of RFID-enabled companies depicted as FMC block diagram. Company-internal and -external systems exchange event data through standardized interfaces of EPCIS as defined by EPCglobal

Table 2.5 Classification of components of RFID information systems

Component	Location	Category	Type
EPCIS repository	Company/SaaS provider	E/I	SW
RFID middleware	Company	I	SW
RFID reader	Company, freight gates, stock, etc.	I	HW
RFID tag	Good	E	HW
Service provider	SaaS provider	E	SW
Discovery service	SaaS provider	E	SW

E external, *HW* hardware, *I* internal, *SW* software. Two-thirds are software components

should be considered as uncontrollable components in terms of security that might be the foundation of further threats [35]. Two thirds of the components given in Table 2.5 are software, whereas I categorized the EPCIS repository as internal and external component equally. In this work, I focus on how to secure internal and external components, i.e. passive RFID tags and EPCIS repositories. The need for focusing on software components arises from the evaluation of components and categories addressed by related work.

Figure 2.4 visualizes the results of my analysis of related work. It depicts the year of publication in relation to the addressed RFID component and quantity of publications. Starting in 2005, it shows that related work dealing with security focuses on the air interface between readers and tags. Due to the limited security capabilities of low-cost tags and uncontrollable vulnerable environments the tag's content can be obtained with various well-researched techniques. For further details please refer to Chap. 4. Moreover, Fig. 2.4 highlights two further

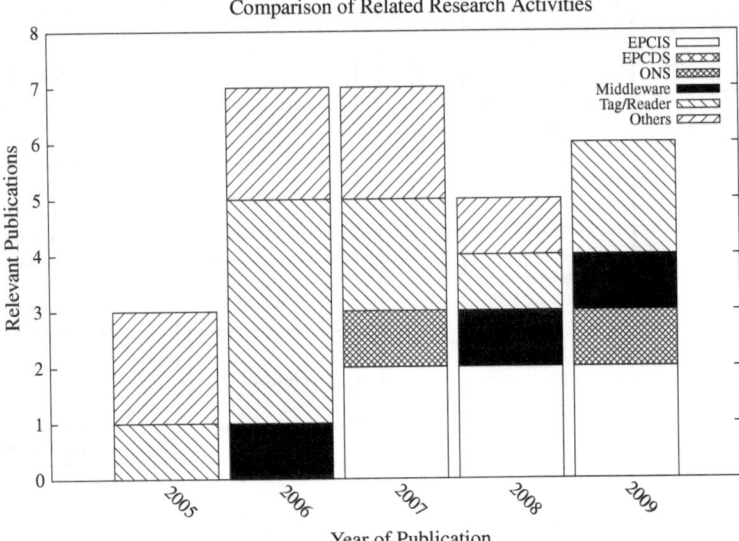

Fig. 2.4 Comparison of related work depicting year of publication (2005–2009) versus addressed component and amount of relevant publications. Until 2007, Publications addressing security of components tags, readers, and their communication dominate. From 2008 on, Work addressing security of software systems, such as EPCIS repositories, middleware, and ONS, dominate. Work addressing the security of EPCDS is not present

characteristics of related work: (a) research activities concerning security of enterprise components started after device-level security was researched and (b) work dealing with security aspects of enterprise components of EPCglobal networks rarely exist in comparison of work addressing the air interface, tags, or reader hardware. Although switching to EPCglobal networks involves new hardware components, e.g. RFID readers for RFID technology or barcode scanner when incorporating visual identification techniques, various software components are also required. Table 2.5 classifies components of RFID-aided supply chains according to the category's location within the supply chain, its access type, and whether it is a hard- or software component. It highlights that the amount of involved enterprise software components, such as EPCIS repository, EPCDS, ONS, etc., is twice the amount of involved hardware components. The majority of involved enterprise software components motivate my research activities on business-level security in the rest of my work.

A similar trend can also be observed for industrial implementation projects, e.g. for product authenticity. For example, the pharmaceutical manufacturer Pfizer started a pilot project to use RFID technology for tracking pharmaceuticals in 2006, but it was not rolled out company-wide, until today [36]. The Metro Future Store initiative aims to improve supply chain management in the last step of supply chain: in retail stores, but most of the examples lack concrete productive implementation [37]. Public discussions about the reasons for stopping these projects are not available. However, concerns about data security and privacy are considered as possible reasons [33]. Initiatives, such as FoeBuD e.V. in Germany, fight for a strict use of RFID tags in industries, e.g. in retail stores [38]. Figure 2.4 depicts that these privacy concerns are addressed by related work for securing RFID-specific enterprise systems starting in 2007. This dissertation contributes by providing security extensions for RFID-specific enterprise software components to increase the acceptance and the future usage of EPCglobal networks.

My dissertation combines access control mechanisms, EPCglobal networks, and RFID technology as individual fields of research. I have analyzed existing related work with respect to each of the research fields focusing on data security and applicability to the given pharmaceutical scenario in Sect. 1.1. Table A.2 in Appendix A.1 classifies related work in the area of access control mechanisms corresponding to their technique specifics and their type of contribution. For example, Abadi and Fournet discuss the dynamic assignment of access rights for programs during their execution and refer to it as HBAC [39]. Edjlali et al. proposed years ago that HBAC "[...] has the potential to significantly expand the set of programs that can be executed without compromising security [...]" [40]. The NIST observed that concrete HBAC implementations are limited, e.g. in terms of real-time analysis of the history [1].

Based on the given components, related work dealing with RFID-specific data security and privacy threats is classified in Tables A.3–A.7. The comparison shows with respect to latest access control approaches a common usage of XML-based approaches for specification of access rights; primarily XACML, which is discussed in the following. Furthermore, there is a two-divided implementation approach for data security in RFID technology. For securing the communication between tag and reader fast hardware-based implementations are incorporated. However, the majority of related work dealing with EPCglobal components proposes software solutions, e.g. when focusing on the aspects authentication or access control. Only a small portion of related work actively makes use of encryption when exchanging data. I assume that most contributions do not consider data security in EPCglobal networks so far due to the missing standardization of the EPCglobal consortium.

References

1. V.C. Hu, D.F. Ferraiolo, D.R. Kuhn, Assessment of Access Control Systems. Interagency Report 7316, National Institute of Standards and Technology (2006)
2. D.F. Ferraiolo, D.R. Kuhn, Role-based access control, in *Proceedings of the 15th NIST National Computer Security Conference* (1992), pp. 554–563
3. A.S. Sodiya, A.S. Onashoga, Components-based access control architecture. Issues Inf. Sci. Inf. Technol. **6**, 699–706 (2009)
4. OASIS Open. eXtensible Access Control Markup Language (XACML) V.2.0, Feb 2005
5. J. Clark, XSL Transformations (XSLT) (1999), http://www.w3.org/TR/xslt. Accessed 8 Mar 2012

6. E. Grummt, M. Schöffel, Verteilte Autorisation in RFID-Ereignissystemen, in *D.A.CH Security: Bestandsaufnahme, Konzepte, Anwendungen, Perspektiven*, ed. by P. Horster (Berlin, 2008) pp. 337–345
7. ODRL Initiative: ODRL V2.0 - XML encoding (2010), http://odrl.net/2.0/WD-ODRL-XML.html. Accessed 8 Mar 2012
8. Global Standards 1: GS1 standards knowledge centre (2011), http://www.gs1.org/gsmp/kc/epcglobal/. Accessed 8 Mar 2012
9. International Organization for Standardization, ISO/IEC 18000: Information Technology—Radio Frequency Identification for Item Management, 2004–2010
10. International Telecommunication Union, ST61 Agreement (2011), http://www.itu.int/ITU-R/terrestrial/broadcast/plans/st61/index.html. Accessed 8 Mar 2012
11. A. Selian, 3G mobile licensing policy: from GSM to IMT-2000—a comparative analysis technical report, International Telecommunication Union (2001)
12. E.C. Jones, C.A. Chung, *RFID in Logistics: A Practical Introduction* (CRC Press, Boca Raton, 2007)
13. K. Finkenzeller, *RFID Handbook: Fundamentals and Applications in Contactless Smart Cards, Radio Frequency Identification and Near-Field Communication*, 2nd edn. (Wiley, New York, 2010)
14. M. Roberti, The history of RFID technology. RFID J. 1–3 (2008)
15. Heydt-Benjamin et al., Vulnerabilities in first-generation RFID-enabled credit cards, in *Financial Cryptography and Data Security*, volume 4886 of Lecture Notes in Computer Science, ed. by S. Dietrich, R. Dhamija (Springer, Berlin, 2007), pp. 2–14
16. Global standards 1: EPCglobal object name service 1.0.1 (2008), http://www.gs1.org/gsmp/kc/epcglobal/ons/ons_1_0_1-standard-20080529.pdf. Accessed 8 Mar 2012
17. Global Standards 1: EPCIS standard 1.0.1 (2007), http://www.gs1.org/gsmp/kc/epcglobal/epcis/epcis_1_0_1-standard-20070921.pdf. Accessed 8 Mar 2012
18. Global Standards 1: discovery services standard (in development) (2011), http://www.gs1.org/gsmp/kc/epcglobal/discovery. Accessed 8 Mar 2012
19. J. Müller, An in-memory discovery service to retrieve track & trace information in a unique identifier network with hierarchical packaging (to appear), Ph.D. thesis, Hasso Plattner Institute, 2012
20. Global Standards 1: EPCglobal certificate profile specification version 1.0 (2010), http://www.gs1.org/gsmp/kc/epcglobal/cert/cert_1_0-standard-20060308.pdf. Accessed 8 Mar 2012
21. Global standards 1: EPCglobal certificate profile specification version 2.0 (2010), http://www.gs1.org/gsmp/kc/epcglobal/cert/cert_2_0-standard-20100610.pdf. Accessed 8 Mar 2012
22. The Institute of Electrical and Electronics Engineers, Inc, Wireless LAN medium access control (MAC) and physical layer (PHY) specifications (2010), http://standards.ieee.org/getieee802/download/802.11z-2010.pdf. Accessed 8 Mar 2012
23. Bundesamt für Sicherheit in der Informationstechnik: BSI TR-03128 EAC-PKI'n für den elektronischen Personalausweis, V. 1.1 (2010), https://www.bsi.bund.de/ContentBSI/Publikationen/TechnischeRichtlinien/tr03128/index_htm.html. Accessed 8 Mar 2012
24. The Institute of Electrical and Electronics Engineers, Inc., EEE standard for local and metropolitan area networks: overview and architecture (2002), http://standards.ieee.org/getieee802/download/802-2001.pdf. Accessed 8 Mar 2012
25. A. Benlian, T. Hess, P. Buxmann, *Software-as-a-Service: Kunden-Anbieterstrategien* (Kundenbedürfnisse und Wertschöpfungsstrukturen, Gabler, 2010)
26. M.-P. Schapranow, M. Lorenz, A. Zeier, H. Plattner, License-based access control in EPCglobal networks, in *Proceedings of 7th European Workshop on Smart Objects: Systems, Technologies and Applications*, VDE, 2011
27. M.-P. Schapranow, ENIAC tutorial: the modulo function (2006), http://www.myhpi.de/~schapran/eniac/modulo. Accessed 8 Mar 2012
28. M.R. Rieback, B. Crispo, A.S. Tanenbaum, The evolution of RFID security. IEEE Pervasive Comput. **5**, 62–69 (2006)

29. B.W. Lampson, Protection, in *Proceedings of 5th Princeton Conference on Information Sciences and Systems* (1971), pp. 437–443
30. European Commission, Recommendation on privacy and data protection in applications supported by radio-frequency identification (2009), http://ec.europa.eu/information_society/policy/rfid/documents/recommendationonrfid2009.pdf. Accessed 8 Mar 2012
31. Federal Office for Information Security, BSI standard 100–3: risk analysis based on IT-Grundschutz V.2.5 (2008)
32. S.L. Garfinkel, A. Juels, R. Pappu, RFID privacy: an overview of problems and proposed solutions. IEEE Secur. Priv. **3**, 34–43 (2005)
33. S. Spiekermann, Privacy enhancing technologies for RFID in retail: an empirical investigation, in *Proceedings of the 9th International Conference on Ubiquitous Computing* (Springer, Berlin, 2007), pp. 56–72
34. E. Bertino, P.A. Bonatti, E. Ferrari, TRBAC: a temporal role-based access control model. ACM Trans. Inf. Syst. Secur. **4**, 191–233 (2001)
35. M.-P. Schapranow, J. Müller, A. Zeier, H. Plattner, Security aspects in vulnerable RFID-aided supply chains, in *Proceedings of 5th European Workshop on RFID Systems and Technologies*, VDE, 2009
36. US Pharmaceuticals Pfizer Inc., Anti-counterfeit drug initiative workshop and vendor display (2006),http://www.fda.gov/OHRMS/DOCKETS/dockets/05n0510/05N-0510-EC21-Attach-1.pdf. Accessed 8 Mar 2012
37. METRO Group, METRO group and RFID (2008), http://www.future-store.org/fsi-internet/get/documents/FSI/multimedia/pdfs/broschueren/RFID%20und%20MG-E-271108-Internet.pdf. Accessed 8 Mar 2012
38. FoeBuD e.V. Die StopRFID-Seiten des FoeBuD e.V. (2012), http://www.foebud.org/rfid/index_html. Accessed 8 Mar 2012
39. M. Abadi, C. Fournet, Access control based on execution history, in *Proceedings of the 10th Annual Network and Distributed System Security, Symposium* (2003), pp. 107–121
40. G. Edjlali, A. Acharya, V. Chaudhary, History-based access control for mobile code, in *Proceedings of 5th Conference on Computer and Communications, Security* (1998), pp. 38–48

Chapter 3
Security in EPCglobal Networks

After the analysis and classification of related work, I deal with specific security requirements for RFID environments in the following. I focus on why business relationships in global supply chains need to be analyzed in detail with respect to security. Furthermore, I show that RFID environments suffer from certain threats that are also known for communication networks. Instead of applying counter-measures to a certain security issue, I motivate the use of a *security matrix* to protect data in RFID-aided supply chains. As a result, I consider security from two perspectives: from a business and a technical perspective. In the following chapter, I introduce a specific modeling approach for integrating event data in existing business processes with respect to data security. Moreover, I present key concepts of in-memory technology, which build the technical foundation of the presented security extensions in the remainder of this work.

Business Relationships in Supply Chains: To address business relationships between supply chain participants, I distinguish between closed and open supply chains. I refer to *closed supply chains* when business relationships are limited to a predefined set of partners, e.g. due to static limitations to enter the market, such as legal regulations. In contrast, I refer to *open supply chains* when supply chain partners are dynamically exchanging goods with each other, e.g. in supply chains for highly standardized products such as electronic components.

Today, closed supply chains exist in various traditional industries, e.g. automotive or energy supplying industries. For example, the automotive industry ensures the quality of their products by excessively testing new products before switching vendors [1]. New vendors need to prepare product samples that are examined by automobile manufacturers before switching suppliers. Furthermore, a degree of process certification is required by vendors to guarantee a certain quality within the manufacturing process [2].

In emerging global supply chains, establishing business relationships with new or unknown parties is a challenging and still open issue. Open supply chains are more likely to emerge more probably in industries dealing with highly standardized and interchangeable ingredients, components, or goods. Standardization helps to specify product properties while enabling supplier switches. Thus, product costs become the

Matthieu-P. Schapranow, *Real-time Security Extensions for EPCglobal Networks*,
In-Memory Data Management Research, DOI: 10.1007/978-3-642-36343-6_3,
© Springer-Verlag Berlin Heidelberg 2014

main differentiator. However, the question arises how to ensure the quality of the product? Holding certain process certificates is a possible indicator for quality and a limitation for counterfeiters to enter the market [2]. It requires trusted certificates, but their issuer might also suffer from faked certificates. In addition, the data flow between supply-chain parties can be analyzed to verify exchanged meta data. This requires full control of all supply chain parties, which is not acceptable for all involved parties due to potential exposure of supplier relationships and an abrupt high level of transparency.

The raising level of globalization will result in more and more open supply chains. Existing local controls, e.g. process certificates can temporarily restrict access of counterfeiters. However, a globally trusted certificate is a challenging and still open problem. The 2009 communiqué of ISO underlines that the organization defines the standards for certification but it is performed by third-party bodies that are not explicitly controlled [3]. As a result, EPCglobal networks need to be extended by qualified security features to guarantee the authenticity of products and supply chain parties. For example, authentication of supply chain parties enables the identification of liable suppliers, e.g. in case of product malfunctions. As a result, the security extensions presented in Chap. 5 contribute to guarantee the integrity of goods in open supply chains built upon EPCglobal networks.

In context of this work, I assume a global RFID-aided supply chain for the pharmaceutical industry. In contrast to traditional regional supply chains with a limited number of participants, e.g. some well-known business partners, an open RFID-aided supply chain results in potentially unlimited participants and intermediate relationships. As a result, the effort for defining individual access rights per inquirer becomes a time-consuming task.

Information Security: The term *security* is not sharply defined in context of EPCglobal networks and RFID technology. I consider EPCglobal systems as an integral part of modern enterprise systems. Thus, I refer to definitions for information security in IT systems and apply them to EPCglobal networks and RFID technology. Information security addresses the aspects confidentiality, integrity, and availability of information [4, 5].

At this point, I distinguish between the terms *data* and *information*. Following Wendt's definitions, the term *data* refers to information that is available in symbols, e.g. letters, bits, signals, etc. and the term *information* or *knowledge* refers to interpreted data, e.g. by human-beings or information systems [6]. In literature the term data protection is often used synonymously for information security. However, in contrast to information security, data protection or data security refers nowadays to data privacy [4].

Confidentiality, Integrity, and Availability: *Confidentiality* supports data protection by restricting readings of data to authorized entities only [7]. *Integrity* of data aims to protect any kind of data manipulation—intended or unintended. The *availability* aspect guarantees access to data when requested by authorized entities.

3.1 Vulnerable Environments

Cables establish the link between two communication peers in traditional communication networks, e.g. in the plain old telephone services or in local area networks. If these wired links are secured against physical access, attackers are typically not able to gain unrecognized access. In wireless communication networks, it is hard to secure communication because data are transmitted via the ether, which can be accessed by malicious attackers without being recognized. RFID technology makes use of both communication media. On the one hand, data are exchanged via traditional wired communication networks, e.g. EPC event is exchanged between EPCIS repositories for authenticity checks of pharmaceutical goods. On the other hand, communication between RFID tag and reader is performed via the ether. Security threats for EPCglobal networks, in particular in combination RFID technology, are defined in Sect. 3.1.1. In addition, attacks of communication networks are mapped to RFID technology and evaluated in Sect. 3.1.2 and security requirements for EPCglobal networks are derived in Sect. 3.1.3. If item-level identifiers are not exchanged via RFID technology, only corresponding wired security issues only exist. However, I focus on RFID since its use introduces additional security threats in contrast to other transmission techniques, such as barcode readers.

Threats of EPCglobal networks as discussed in Sect. 3.1.1 and attacks focusing on RFID technology as discussed in Sect. 3.1.2 are summarized in Table 3.1.

Data Integrity: Data protection in context of communication networks refers to multiple aspects. A defined set of data must remain valid during the lifetime of its associated product. Furthermore, it must be ensured that all authorized supply chain parties can access data at any time without unexpected manipulations or modifications [8]. This kind of data protection is referred to as data integrity. It ensures that third parties are not able to modify data during its lifecycle—expectedly or unexpectedly.

Data Quality: Another aspect of data protection is *data quality*. It highlights the issue that data describing a given item is not always processed correctly [8]. Radio technology suffers from various aspects that can influence the transmission quality.

Table 3.1 Classification of security threats and possible attacks in EPCglobal networks with respect to their location in the supply chain. Most attacks correspond to threat *T6*, which involves *RFID* tags and *EPCIS* repositories

Th.	Attacks	Loc.	Involved components	Actors
T1	A3	I, O, T	EPC, RFID Tag	A, R
T2	A3	I	EPCDS, EPCIS	C, R
T3	A1, A3	O, T	EPC, RFID Tag	A
T4	A3	I, T	EPC	C, R
T5	A3	I	EPCIS	R
T6	A2, A3, A4, A5, A6, A7	I, O, T	EPC, EPCIS, RFID Tag	A, C

A = Attacker, *C* = Counterfeiter, *I* = Inside the Supply Chain, *Loc.* = Location, *O* = Outside the Supply Chain, *R* = Competitor, *T* = Transition Zone of the Supply Chain, *Th.* = Threat

Multiple readers and tags communicating simultaneously can limit coverage of radio waves and influence the quality of read data. Data quality is important for tracking and tracing since assumptions about the path of goods within the supply chain are incorporated in verification of product authenticity. For instance, certain readers have to be passed in a defined order to ensure that a product was handled by authorized intermediaries only. Reduced data quality influences available data for authenticity checks of products.

3.1.1 Threats of RFID-Aided Supply Chains

Figure 3.1 depicts a classification of supply chain parties and possible attacks. It consists of suppliers, i.e. manufacturers that create goods, manufacturers that assemble goods, wholesalers, retailers, and customers. In addition, it depicts three categories of malicious actors: (a) competitors within the supply chain, (b) counterfeiter and (c) attackers outside of the supply chain. Correspondingly to the classification of Garfinkel et al. actors are assigned to classes [9]. Due to the variety of involved actors in supply chains, specific security issues exist. The following classification combines security issues of supply chains with issues of EPCglobal networks.

T1 Implicit Product Identification: The EPC references the product's manufacturer and the class of the product. For example, the SGTIN looks like `urn:epc:id:sgtin:CompanyPrefix.ItemReference.Serial-Number` as defined by EPCglobal [10, Sect. 6.3.1]. If the EPC is stored on a RFID tag, it can be read from distance without establishing a direct line of sight. Thus, the manufacturing company and the class of the product can be derived even when there is no direct access to the product. Furthermore, tagged products in transportations units can be derived by thefts by scanning their RFID tag with commodity readers. As a result, protection of on-tag data needs to be considered with respect to authorized parties. For further details please refer to Chap. 4.

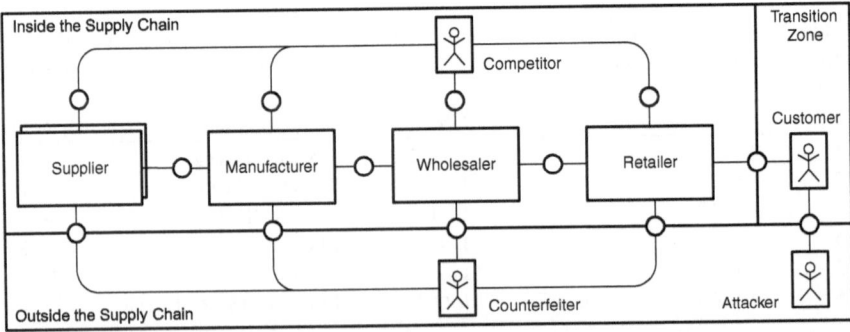

Fig. 3.1 FMC block diagram depicting classification of supply chain parties and possible attacks

T2 Supplier Relationships: Querying the EPCDS or EPCIS repository of involved supply chain parties within the supply chain is the basis to reconstruct a product's full path through the supply chain. On the one hand, this is the basis for the anti-counterfeiting service provider. On the other hand, business relationships, e.g. intermediate wholesalers, are exposed when returning a full list of EPCIS repositories of supply chain parties that handled the queried product. Furthermore, competitors could query details about a guessed EPC of a potential product ingredient. If the EPCIS repository of the manufacturer returns any details, it exposes implicitly the business relationship with the supplier and possible product ingredients [11].

T3 Customer Privacy: Due to the unique serial number stored in EPCs, customers can be tracked when they hold a product equipped with a functional tag [12]. Manufacturer and attackers can associate customers with products they bought, e.g. during verification of the product's authenticity. This exposes the customer's privacy.

T4 Customer Relationships: The unique serial of the EPC used for item-level identification exposes relationships of supply chain parties that handled the good. For example, relationships between individual supply chain parties within the supply chain or with customers in the transition zone of the supply chain are affected by this issue. This has a major impact on the integrity of the supply chain.

T5 Industrial Espionage: Competitors can query the EPCIS to receive details about the processing time. For example, the time between product shipment and receipt can be derived. This measure can be used as indicator for selling rate, production time, or supply shortages and occurs within the supply chain. Furthermore, if event data is exchanged in clear text, its content can be eavesdropped. For example, external parties can analyze process steps involving the handled product.

T6 Counterfeit Injection: Unique identification of products reduces the possibility of counterfeit injection. However, reusing a stolen tag on a counterfeited product, guessing a valid EPC code, or skimming of EPCs from authentic products can be misused for counterfeit injecting. Injecting faked EPCs into EPCIS repositories result can be used to make a faked product authentic from the EPCIS repository's perspective. Intercepting the communication between EPCIS and querying party can be used to return authentic details for faked products.

These brief examples highlight privacy concerns and security threats that arise in EPCglobal networks when fine-grained event data are automatically exchanged. On the one hand, controlling access to event data is the first step to prevent the aforementioned issues. On the other hand, restricting access to a subset of event data does not prevent its combination. From my perspective, the combination of event data is the basis to derive business secrets and business relationships.

3.1.2 Attacks Scenarios

In the following section, attacks of communication networks are presented and their potential impacts on RFID-aided supply chains are derived.

A1 Malicious RFID Readers: Data protection threats in RFID-aided supply chains are comparable to existing pendants in Wi-Fi networks. I assume that additional security mechanisms will be introduced to harden the resistance of RFID against manipulated RFID readers. Currently, it is possible to use commodity readers to access passive low-cost tags that are, for example, integrated in passports or driver's licenses [13].

For the pharmaceutical scenario defined in Sect. 1.1, this introduces the following issues. EPCs can be obtained without having physical access to the carrying tags. As a result, the EPC of a blister packet stored on a RFID tag can be read out after the customer has left the pharmacy. The holder of a tag does not know that a read attempt occurred. Furthermore, the knowledge that a particular customer holds a specific tag can be misused to track customers, too. These are customer privacy threats as defined by threat T3. From the customer's point of view, the tags needs to be disabled before leaving the pharmacy to ensure personal privacy.

A2 Tampered RFID Tags: Manipulating RFID-aided supply chains does not mandatorily involve attacking readers. Often it is sufficient to irritate the tag's function, e.g. by sending manipulated data or to shield tags from readers. With the help of a special wireless interface, an attacker can emit a recorded tag transmission to an incoming stimulus by a reader. In context of the pharmaceutical scenario, it allows exchange of an authentic product by a manipulated one while simulating the tag's behavior of the authentic product. Once the response of an authentic pallet was recorded it can be replayed many times. It may be sufficient that a single corrupted tag escorts a pallet of multiple items without the need for integrating it into the pallet itself. This threat can be misused to inject counterfeits into the supply chain as defined by threat T6.

A3 Man-In-The-Middle Attack: The Man-In-The-Middle (MITM) attack has been known in communication networks for years [14]. Data exchanged between two peers A and B is transmitted through different routes. Routes are dynamically set-up by the incorporated communication protocol. Once an attacker is controlling one node on the route or is able to influence the connection setup process through a specific route, the network traffic between A and B can be filtered. MITM attacks are used to gain login information. In context of the EPCglobal networks, they can be performed in context of all mentioned threats.

The detection of unauthorized read events becomes very important, especially when using security-enhanced tags. The EPCglobal standard defines a kill command, which can be issued by sending a freely programmable 2×16-bit kill PIN [15]. Although this is an irreversible action, it is interesting for attackers to obtain the kill PIN. Programming hundreds, thousands or hundreds of thousands tags with a dedicated kill PIN is a time-consuming operation. Every tag has to be programmed with a unique kill PIN. The kill PIN has to be stored in a company meta data repository connecting it with the corresponding EPC. Additionally, during tag programming it has to be ensured that a strong PRN generator is used for generation of the kill PIN, i.e. duplicates have to be omitted. Otherwise, gathering a single kill PIN might expose kill PINs of a certain product group or company. Attackers could disable tags of a complete delivery, which would result in blocked business processes that depend on the correct functionality of the tags.

In RFID-aided supply chains transportation routes of items are similar to routes in communication networks. Comparable to unsecured wireless connections, which can be accessed over a long distance, RFID technology suffers from very similar threats. RFID readers can be placed anywhere to acquire data of passing tags, e.g. in context of threat T4 or T2 . The current owner of a product equipped with a RFID tag is not able to recognize read attempts without special equipment. Let us assume the pharmaceutical scenario given in Sect. 1.1. At the point of sale in the pharmacy, the kill command is issued to disable the RFID tag of a pharmaceutical product. The pharmacy authenticates itself to the supplier, checks whether the current product is authentic and queries for the specific kill PIN. Issuing the kill command ensures the customer's privacy by making it impossible to draw any mappings between product and customer after leaving the pharmacy, e.g. to prevent threat T3.

A4 Cloning and Spoofing: Low-cost passive RFID tags, which are primarily used for tracking and tracing scenarios, are neither equipped with computational power nor any security equipment as described in Sect. 2.2. Thus, any third party can access the tag's content with commodity reader devices. *Cloning* is the process of creating a complete copy of an original tag including the contained EPC. Copying an entire tag is the basis for injecting counterfeits into the supply chain as defined by threat T6. Once an existing product is replaced by a counterfeit its meta data history is valid from the point of view of any querying party. A cloned tag inherits the virtual product history of its original tag pendant.

Spoofing in terms of RFID—also known as masquerading or identity theft— exploits a trusted relationship between two peers [16]. It is the process of influencing a RFID reader, which assumes to receive the EPC of a specific tag, while the original tag is absent. Spoofing can be achieved by cloning the original tag or by simulating a tag containing a virtual non-existing EPC. It is the basis for injecting counterfeits as defined by threat T6.

The EPCglobal tag standard defines unique product identification, but it does not define how to assign serial numbers [10]. If serial numbers are assigned in a strictly linear order, attackers can derive faked ones by guessing. To reduce the possibility of serial number guessing a proper PRN generator needs to calculate new serial numbers for EPCs. This way, spoofed EPCs can be detected if a non-valid EPC is checked against the vendor's list of valid EPCs. This security issue has already been recognized by the industry. For example,

Bayer Technology Services recently announced a product providing an algorithm for unique random number generation of serials for use in track and trace scenarios [17].

A5 Replay Attack: In terms of communication networks replay attacks are prepared by MITM attacks [18]. A third party listens to the conversation of two peers. Once a certain information is gathered, the attacker reuses it, e.g. for logging into a secured system. Computer systems can be protected against replay attacks, e.g. by using One-Time Passwords (OTPs). Their validity is limited for a one-time use only [19].

In RFID-aided supply chains, replay attacks can occur if products tagged with the same tag pass reader gates succeeding times, e.g. hours or days after the original tag passed in context of counterfeit injection as defined by threat T6. A manifestation in the pharmaceutical scenario is an EPC of a pharmaceutical product that is scanned during goods receipt multiple times at the site of the same vendor. Juels proposes the use of so-called pseudonyms, which are randomly changed after each read request [20]. Pseudonyms work in a similar way like OTPs. In addition, they influence the uniqueness of the exchanged data. As a result, without concrete knowledge of incorporated pseudonyms, the exchanged data cannot be derived. As a result, pseudonyms reduce replay attacks and traceability of tags by eavesdroppers while the decoded EPC remains unchanged.

A6 Controlled Signal Interferences: Signal interferences are issues, which prevent proper tag reading. RFID technology uses different bands for wireless communication as described in Sect. 2.2. Comparable to any kind of radio communication, the quality of RFID communication depends on the used band. If multiple communication attempts occur simultaneously, transmission quality degrades. Various liquids and metals, such as lead or aluminium shield radio waves. As a result, tags cannot be read successfully or the data quality of the response degrades.

It is possible to overlay radio waves by triggering controlled interferences with transmissions of higher amplitude. Attackers can hide the existence of spoofed tags by provoking controlled interferences. This technique can be used to hide counterfeits on its way as defined by threat T6.

A7 Data Encryption: Communication via unreliable networks can be secured by using data encryption. In Wi-Fi networks encryption standards are used, e.g. TKIP or AES [21]. Data encryption prevents attackers from gathering data out of an encrypted communication stream. It is based on generating PRN out of a large domain for use as encryption keys. It is referred to as a secure encryption as long as no brute-force attack is able to obtain encrypted data in appropriate time. With increasing computational power, encryption standards become weak, such as the Data Encryption Standard (DES) [22]. Cloning an encrypted RFID tag results in a perfect copy of the original. Although the encrypting data on tag prevents attackers from reading the EPC in clear text, the perfect clone acts identically to its original pendant. As a result, encryption in context of RFID technology leaves the issues cloning and spoofing still open. As a result, encryption does not prevent threat T6 in context of EPCglobal networks [23].

3.1.3 Security Requirements

After having discussed selected threats for RFID systems, I define concrete data security requirements for IT systems in context of EPCglobal networks. From a system engineering's point of view, these requirements build the security blueprint during the design phase for the upcoming implementation. I focus on functional and non-functional system requirements.

Functional requirements describe how certain aspects of security extensions should react in response to concrete stimulus and how they should behave in certain situations whereas non-functional requirements define constraints that apply to the complete security extensions focusing on provided functions and services [24, Sect. 6.1.].

Functional Requirements: In the following, I discuss a selected list of functional requirements for security extension of EPCglobal networks. They are driven by the need for verification of goods without significant latency in business processes, e.g. when dealing with fast-moving goods. Since response time behavior as described in Hyp. 1 is essential for the applicability of my security extensions, I consider response time as a functional requirement in contrast to existing literature.

F1 **Response Time:** From the business' perspective, applying security extensions must not result in significant delays of existing business processes. As a concrete example, the goods receipt process should be used as a motivation in the following. With respect to my research Hyp.1, an upper threshold of two seconds processing time must not be exceeded.

F2 **Control Access:** Security extensions must control access to event data.

F3 **Authenticated Users:** Security extensions need to grant access to authenticated users only.

F4 **Querying Parties:** Keeping track of querying parties is important in case of data exposure. Any security extension should be aware of the querying party, date, and time when certain data were exposed to embank potential data leakages.

F5 **Data Minimalism:** Querying parties should access only the data that is required to fulfill their tasks [4]. Security extensions should follow the principle of data minimalism by granting access only to relevant data portions. As a result, the inquirer needs to be able to specify, which fraction of data should be returned.

F6 **Filter Data:** Security extensions need to filter the result sets to control data access and to enforce the principle of data minimalism. The result set needs to be filtered to remove protected and sensitive data that is specified as inappropriate for the given inquirer.

Nonfunctional Requirements: The following constraints describe non-functional requirements for security extension of EPCglobal networks. These requirements are driven by the need for affecting the performance of existing business processes at a minimum.

N1 Processing Load: From an operational perspective, security extensions result in additional processing requirements. Increased computational demands require additional hardware at the site of involved supply chain participants that handle many products, e.g. manufacturers and wholesalers. Thus, security extensions should keep requirements for additional computational power as low as possible.

N2 Maintainability: The regular maintenance of access rights is a complex and time-consuming task in IT systems with a predefined number of users and roles. From the engineering perspective, a supply chain consists of a huge number of parties that do not known each other. I consider maintaining individual access rights for all parties as a time-consuming and complex job. Since access rights need to be granted before event data are exchanged, manually managing access rights delays business process that build on the automatic exchange of event data. Security extensions for EPCglobal networks need to automatically assign access rights for unknown supply chain parties on an individual basis.

N3 Ease of Configuration: In terms of configuration, a PAP needs to be provided for defining access rights, rules, etc. It needs to provide a configuration platform that supports the user in testing, modeling, verifying, and configuring access rights and rules.

N4 Ease of Integration: Migrating to a new software or release is a complex and time-consuming task. For example, changing data formats involves processing of all data involved. As a result, security extensions should optimize migration efforts with respect to expected downtime and need for processing of current data in use.

3.2 Modeling and Simulation

EPCglobal networks result in individual meta data for all handled goods. A prerequisite for securing EPCglobal networks is a clear understanding of supply chain participants, their interactions, and the impact on good's meta data. In the following section, I introduce a formal model for RFID-aided supply chains with focus on the flow of handled goods and relevant actions of involved supply chain participants. It is the basis for precise modeling and simulation of EPCglobal networks. For research purposes, I have developed a configurable, discrete supply chain simulator for EPCglobal networks, which generates realistic event data for the pharmaceutical supply chain scenario discussed in Sect. 1.1.

3.2.1 Formal Model for RFID-Aided Supply Chains

For formal analysis of RFID-aided supply chains, real-world business scenarios need to be abstracted in terms of complexity, functionality, and entities. Since data and event flow are of special interest, creating a model of them is the foundation of further security analysis. In contrast to traditional supply chain modeling that aims to optimize transportation routes and focuses on the flow of goods, the presented model focuses on data and event flow in RFID-aided supply chains [25].

From a good's perspective, various operations are performed on its path throughout the supply chain. Some operations result in event generation as a side effect, e.g. goods receipt or goods shipment as depicted in Fig. 3.2. In terms of product verification and validation of its path, these events are essential since they map goods' real-world movements to IT systems and build the basis for analytical processes, e.g. anti-counterfeiting [26].

Entity Coupling
A tight coupling of entities is achieved by an object association, which is introduced by the *entity coupling* as defined in Eq. 3.1; its inverse *decoupling* function is defined in Eq. 3.2. Equation 3.3 defines the entity coupling of epc_i and d_i, which is referred to as tag_i. All entities are also softly sharing the same index i.

$$\boxplus: (b_1, b_2) \mapsto b_3 \tag{3.1}$$

$$\boxminus: (b_3) \mapsto \{b_1, b_2\} \tag{3.2}$$

$$tag_i = epc_i \boxplus d_i \tag{3.3}$$

$$hu_i = tag_i \boxplus p_i \tag{3.4}$$

Belongs-to Relationship
An individual of a class of entities b is precisely identified by an index i as b_i. All related entities for a concrete b_i are referred to as *belongs to* b_i by using the same index i. In contrast to entity coupling the *belongs-to relationship* does not connect entities with each other during their lifecycles. It is a soft relationship for identification purposes only. In other words: b_i is in a belongs-to relationship with a_i,

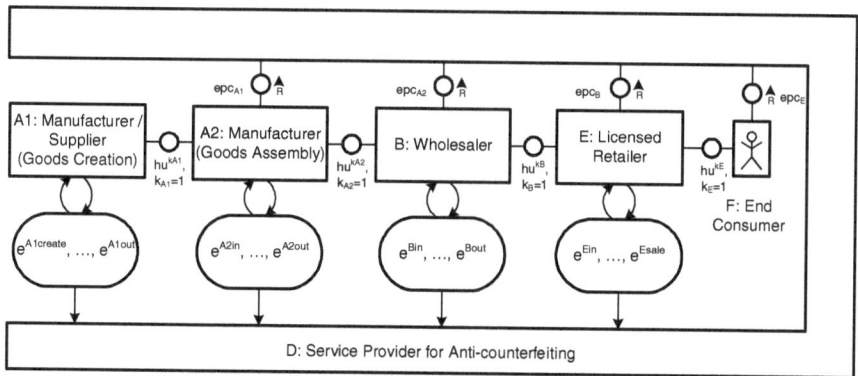

Fig. 3.2 Formal model for the interaction of supply chain parties in EPCglobal networks. Manufacturers perform either goods creation or goods assembly. Event data of associated goods are stored in local EPCIS repositories of each supply chain party

e.g. b_i is created during the product lifecycle of a_i as a result of a processing step. For instance, Eq. 3.3 shows that epc_i and d_i belong to tag_i.

Entity Degree
I define the *entity degree* k for a class of entities b in Eq. 3.5 as the number of boxing operations performed on an entity. For $k = 0$, I refer to $b^0 = b$ as the *atomic* entity, i.e. the product itself since no more unboxing operations can be performed on it.

$$b^k, k \in \{x \in \mathbb{N} | 0 \leq x \leq 5\} \tag{3.5}$$

Entity Handling Unit
I define the following valid values for the entity degree following the reference model for supply chains by Vilkov and Weiß [27]. This mapping shows k and its corresponding physical representations, which I refer to as *entity handling unit* hu_i^k of degree k as follows:

k = 0: The atomic entity b_i, i.e. the product itself,
k = 1: A product package, which holds b_i,
k = 2: A transport package, e.g. a paper box,
k = 3: A re-useable transport package, e.g. a pallet or a skeleton,
k = 4: A transport container, e.g. for transportation on ships or aircrafts, and
k = 5: A freight vehicle, e.g. aircraft, ship, or truck.

Entity Boxing and Unboxing
I introduce the *boxing* operation $\boxdot$ in Eq. 3.6, which is used to define a concrete handling unit hu_j identified by j that consists of items with differing k as

$$hu_j^{k_j}, k_j = 1 + max(\{k_h, \ldots, k_i\}), h, i, j \in \mathbb{N}^+$$

by applying $\boxdot$ to a set of $\{hu_h^{k_h}, \ldots, hu_i^{k_i}\}, k < 5$. Instead of naming all contained handling units, the formal representation is simplified to the resulting $hu_j^{k_j}$. The inverse *unboxing* operation $\boxplus$ is defined by Eq. 3.7 and can be applied to all $hu_j^{k_j}$ with $k_j > 0$.

$$\boxdot : \{hu_h^{k_h}, \ldots, hu_i^{k_i}\} \mapsto hu_j^{k_j}\left(\{hu_h^{k_h}, \ldots, hu_i^{k_i}\}\right) \tag{3.6}$$

$$\boxplus : hu_j^{k_j}\left(\{hu_h^{k_h}, \ldots, hu_i^{k_i}\}\right) \mapsto \{u_h^{k_h}, \ldots, hu_i^{k_i}\} \tag{3.7}$$

Entity Events
Events are used to establish the product's virtual history. An *entity event* is defined as quart-tuple of values that are used to identify the product in space and time. Therefore, the EPC epc_i describing the product uniquely, the capture timestamp t^{ρ_τ}, the location loc^{ρ_τ}, and the performed business action ba^{ρ_τ} are recorded. The latter is recorded to store details for plausibility checks, such as anti-counterfeiting. Equation 3.8 defines the set of entity events E^ρ as

$$E^\rho = \{e_i^{\rho_\tau} | \rho \in \{A, \ldots, E\}, \tau \in \{in, \ldots, \phi, \ldots, out\}\}$$

with ρ describing the supply chain roles $A, \ldots, E$ and τ describing the locations at the current supply chain role, e.g. *in* or *out*.

$$e_i^{\rho_\tau} = (epc_i, t^{\rho_\tau}, loc^{\rho_\tau}, ba^{\rho_\tau}) \tag{3.8}$$

Roles: I agree on the role concept for RFID-aided supply chains and enhance it by introducing a formal representation for involved data entities to derive a *virtual product history* [27]. I define the virtual product history *PH* for a product p_i in Eq. 3.9 as the chronologically ordered set of event data contributed by all participants handling a certain p_i during the product lifecycle in the supply chain. This set of event data is used to derive product details, such as logistic routes or throughput timings, for a certain customer, route, or vendor.

$$PH(p_i) = \left\{e^{\rho_\tau} | t^{\rho_{i\tau_i}} < t^{\rho_{j\tau_j}}, i < j \right\} \tag{3.9}$$

Supply chain roles and involved data entities of RFID-aided supply chains are modeled with reference to pharmaceutical scenario depicted in Fig. 1.1. It highlights the special involvement of a service provider for anti-counterfeiting accessing the distributed event repositories of all supply chain participants that handled a certain good.

Role A: Manufacturer
The manufacturer role performs two separate tasks: goods assembly and goods creation. *Goods assembly* combines existing ingredients from suppliers to create a complete new product. *Goods creation* brings products alive, i.e. the manufacturer acts as supplier, e.g. by providing chemical ingredients. I refer to a *supplier* as a manufacturer that is performing goods creation. In terms of the goods assembly, the manufacturer acts as a consumer of ingredients provided by supplier. Thus, the manufacturer acts similarly to the end consumer and consumes the ingredient. In context of EPCglobal networks, the manufacturer needs to create and maintain meta data of goods to establish a digital representation of its produced goods.

The following steps are only required once a new product is created and they are not performed for goods assembly.

A_1^*: Equip the product p_i with a proper RFID tag tag_i to create the handling unit hu_i, i.e. the physical connection between the product and its tag as defined in Eq. 3.4.

A_2^*: Determine the next available unique EPC epc_i from the manufacturer's EPC repository for product p_i.

A_3^*: Write the initial content epc_i and optional data d_i, such as ACLs, to the RFID tag. d_i may contain security details or ACLs. Eq. 3.3 introduces the entity coupling of epc_i and d_i. I refer to it as tag_i because it describes the content of the RFID tag.

A_4^*: Establish the virtual product history for p_i starting at timestamp $t^{A_{create}}$ by storing the creation event in the manufacturer's event repository. Eq. 3.8 defines for $\rho = A, \tau = create \exists e^{A_{create}}$ the creation event.

Continue the process on the manufacturer's site and capture events with the involvement of hu_i, e.g. its movements in the warehouse or to the assembly line, as follows.

A_5: Capture all entity events

$$\{e^{A_\alpha}, \ldots, e^{A_\phi}, \ldots, e^{A_{out}}\}$$

defining the path of hu_i at manufacturer locations

$$\{loc^{A_\alpha}, \ldots, loc^{A_\phi}, \ldots, loc^{A_{out}}\}.$$

Equation 3.8 defines for $\rho = A, \tau = out \exists e^{A_{out}}$ the *out* event at the location $loc^{A_{out}}$ of the manufacturer.

Table 3.2 contains the data entities for the corresponding supply chain role separated in IN, INTERN, and OUT, which describe the following aspects:

- IN: describes the set of incoming entities, e.g. a handling unit $hu_i^{k_i}$,
- INTERN: describes a set of events, which is stored at the role's EPCIS event repository also after the handling unit has left the location, and
- OUT: describes the set of outgoing entities, e.g. a handling unit or an empty set $\emptyset$ when the handling unit is consumed.

If the manufacturer is performing goods assembly an existing handling unit $hu_i^{k_i}$ arrives, the manufacturer creates a new product while the incoming handling unit is consumed. $PH_i(hu_i^{k_i})$ of the incoming handling unit ends and is documented with the corresponding *consume* event. For the new product's handling unit $hu_j^{k_j}$ a new $PH_j(hu_j^1)$ is initiated.

Table 3.2 contains the data entities as defined by Eq. 3.8 for $\rho = A, \tau \in \{in, \ldots, consume\}$ for the manufacturer for goods assembly. In case of goods creation no input values exist and $PH_j(hu_j^1)$ of the new handling unit is initiated with the corresponding *create* event. Events defined by Eq. 3.8 for $\rho = A, \tau \in \{create, \ldots, out\}$ are added to its *PH*.

The manufacturer is modeled as a state transformation actor in terms of data, i.e. the function *manufacturer* given in Eq. 3.10 describes the product creation process.

$$manufacturer : \emptyset \mapsto hu_i^1. \tag{3.10}$$

Role B: Wholesaler
The wholesaler's task is to process products for delivery to individual retailers. In context of the RFID-aided supply chain the following additional tasks need to be performed.

Table 3.2 Product and data flows of involved supply chain roles

Role	|IN|	|INTERN|	|OUT|
Manufacturer (good assembly)	$hu_i^{k_i}$	$\bigcup_{\tau=in}^{consume} e_i^{A_\tau}$	$\varnothing$
Manufacturer (good creation)	$\varnothing$	$\bigcup_{\tau=create}^{out} e_i^{A_\tau}$	$hu_i^{k_i}$
Wholesaler	$hu_h^{k_h}, k_h \geq 1$	$\bigcup\left\{\bigcup_{\tau=in}^{\phi} e_h^{B_\tau}, \bigcup_{\tau=\phi}^{out} e_i^{C_\tau}\right\}$	$hu_i^{k_i}, k_i \geq 1$
Logistics provider	$hu_i^{k_i}, k_i \geq 1$	$\bigcup_{\tau=in}^{out} e_i^{C_\tau}$	$hu_i^{k_i}, k_i \geq 1$
Service provider	epc_i	$\{e_i^{p_\tau}, auth\}$	$(epc_i, auth)$
Retailer	$hu_h^{k_h}, k_h \geq 1$	$\bigcup\left\{\bigcup_{\tau=in}^{\phi} e_h^{E_\tau}, \bigcup_{\tau=\phi}^{sale} e_i^{E_\tau}\right\}$	$hu_i^{k_i}, k_i = 0$
End consumer	$hu_i^{k_i}$	$\varnothing$	$\varnothing$

IN = Incoming entities, *INTERN* = Internal events, *OUT* = Outgoing entities, *auth* $\in \{a, c, u\}$

B_1: Capture the goods receipt event e_{in}^B of hu_h^k as defined by Eq. 3.8 for $\rho = B, \tau = in$.

B_2: Capture good receipt events within the wholesaler, e.g. repacking, placing, etc. The set of events E^B is defined by Eq. 3.8 as

$$E^B = \{e_i^{\rho_\tau} | \rho = B, \tau \in \{\alpha, \ldots, \phi, \ldots, \beta\}\}$$

with τ describing intermediate locations at the wholesaler's site. All captured entity events are stored in the event repository of the wholesaler.

B_3: Comparable to the goods receipt the goods shipment is performed. The outgoing event $e^{B_{out}}$ defined by Eq. 3.8 for $\rho = B, \tau = out$ is stored in the event repository.

At the wholesaler's site $hu_h^{k_h}$ is repacked to $hu_i^{k_i}$. Movements of $hu_h^{k_h}$ and $hu_i^{k_i}$ are captured as events as given in Table 3.2. The entity degree k may change depending on the used medium for further transportation. I define a function *wholesaler* in Eq. 3.11.

$$wholesaler : hu_h^{k_h} \mapsto hu_i^{k_i} \tag{3.11}$$

Role C: Logistics Provider

Logistics providers are responsible for transportation of handling units $hu_h^{k_h}$, i.e. moving them from a location $loc^{\rho_{1out}}$ to another location $loc^{\rho_{2in}}$ with $\rho \in \{A, B, E, F\}$. On the route various intermediate locations

$$\left\{loc^{C_{in}}, \ldots, loc^{C_\alpha}, \ldots, loc^{C_\phi}, \ldots, loc^{C_{out}}\right\}$$

are passed. The transportation is performed in a certain transportation time t^C defined by Eq. 3.12.

$$t^C = t^{\rho_{2in}} - t^{\rho_{1out}}. \tag{3.12}$$

The logistics provider exposes details for tracking of goods, which involves captured events at $loc^{C_{in}}$ and $loc^{C_{out}}$. If the logistics provider additionally exposes details about intermediate locations $\{loc^{C_\alpha}, \ldots, loc^{C_\phi}\}$ I refer to it as a logistics provider with real-time tracking capabilities [28]. A logistics provider in context of an RFID-aided supply chain performs the following tasks.

C_1: Capture all events

$$\left\{ e^{C_{in}}, \ldots, e^{C_\alpha}, \ldots, e^{C_\phi}, \ldots, e^{C_{out}} \right\}$$

defining the path of $hu_h^{k_h}$ in the supply chain for $\rho \in \{A, B, E, F\}$:

$$\left\{ loc^{\rho_{1out}}, \ldots, e^{C_{in}}, \ldots, e^{C_{out}}, \ldots, loc^{\rho_{2in}} \right\}.$$

Equation 3.8 defines for $\rho = C, \tau = in \exists e^{C_{in}}$, i.e. the first event for the logistics provider at the pickup location $loc^{\rho_{1out}}$.

The following tasks are only executed when transportation requires boxing or unboxing of $hu_i^{k_i}$.

C_{2a}^*: In case of *boxing* create a new handling unit

$$hu_i^{k_i}\left(\left\{ hu_{h_1}^{k_{h_1}}, \ldots, hu_{h_n}^{k_{h_n}} \right\} \right) = \Box \left\{ hu_{h_1}^{k_{h_1}}, \ldots, hu_{h_n}^{k_{h_n}} \right\},$$

capture events with business action *boxing* $\forall hu_h^{k_h}$, and mark them as being contained in $hu_i^{k_i}$.

C_{2b}^*: In case of *unboxing* of $hu_h^{k_h}$

$$\boxminus hu_h^{k_h}\left(\left\{ hu_{i_1}^{k_{i_1}}, \ldots, hu_{i_n}^{k_{i_n}} \right\} \right),$$

capture unboxing events $\forall hu_i^{k_i}$ that are contained within $hu_h^{k_h}$ and mark it as cleared.

The following task is required for all handling units.

C_3 : Equation 3.8 defines for $\rho = C, \tau = out \exists e^{C_{out}}$, which defines the *out* event for the logistics provider at the drop-off location $e^{\rho_{2in}}$.

Incoming handling units $hu_i^{k_i}$ are transported from their picking location $loc^{\rho_{1out}}$ to their destinations $loc^{\rho_{2in}}$. The logistics provider can perform various boxing or unboxing operations for its purposes. After transportation, the incoming $hu_i^{k_i}$ is available at the drop-off location in its original representation. I define a corresponding function *logistics* in Eq. 3.13.

$$logistics : hu_i^{k_i} \overset{1}{\longmapsto} hu_i^{k_i} \tag{3.13}$$

Role D: Service Provider

The service provider performs specific tasks that are not performed by any other role. For example, it is responsible for anti-counterfeiting, e.g. by performing plausibility checks on the virtual product history with the help of a certain epc_i. Therefore, it is necessary to access the set of events associated with a certain product p_i to reconstruct the virtual product history. The following task is required to perform counterfeit detection.

D_1: I assume that an epc_i uniquely identifies the corresponding p_i. Therefore, I derive the virtual product history for p_i by acquiring all events to build $PH(p_i)$ as defined in Eq. 3.9.

Counterfeit detection is performed with the help of the provided EPC epc_i. I define a function $service_{anti-counterfeiting}$ in Eq. 3.14 performing checks with the help of a given epc_i. It returns either one of the results authentic a, counterfeit c, or unknown u.

$$service_{anti-counterfeiting} : epc_i \mapsto (epc_i, \{a, c, u\}) \qquad (3.14)$$

The service provider returns the value c for a detected counterfeit and the physical product is removed from the supply chain for further investigations. If the virtual product history is valid, the return value is a for authentic. If the outcome of the counterfeit detection cannot be derived automatically, e.g. in case of network partitioning or temporary failures, u for unknown is returned to indicate the need for manual processing. Eq. 3.8 defines all counterfeit detection events as

$$\{e_i^{\tau_p} | \tau, \rho \text{ defined by requester}, ba = \text{counterfeit detection}\},$$

which are locally stored by the service provider as given in Table 3.2.

Role E: Licensed Retailer

The licensed retailer receives $hu_h^{k_h}$ via a logistics provider either from manufacturers, dealers, or wholesalers. Retailers may use either their local event repository for storing captured events or a centralized hosted event repository, which is available on a SaaS subscription basis [29]. The retailer's task is to unpack $hu_h^{k_h}$ and sell its content to end consumers or to other retailers.

E_1: Receive handling unit and capture the goods receipt event as defined by Eq. 3.8 for $\rho = E, \tau = in$.

E_2: Unpack received handling unit $hu_h^{k_h}$ recursively and process contained handling units $hu_i^{k_i}$ individually, i.e. store all events defined by Eq. 3.8 for $\rho = E, \tau \in \{in, \ldots, \phi, \ldots, \beta\}$ in the event repository.

E_3: Capture the *sale* event defined by Eq. 3.8 for $\rho = E, \tau = sale$.

Incoming handling units $hu_h^{k_h}$ are processed and hu_i^1 is sold to other retailers or end consumers as given in Table 3.2. I define a function *retailer* in Eq. 3.15.

$$retailer : hu_h^{k_h} \mapsto hu_i^1 \qquad (3.15)$$

Role F: End Consumer

The supply chain role end consumer occurs only once for a product and defines the sink for a certain product, i.e. end consumer does not perform any tasks in terms of RFID-aided supply chains.

The consumer receives hu_i^1 and removes it from the supply chain as given in Table 3.2. Special supply chain actions, such as product recalls or warranty cases, are not addressed in this thesis for clarity reasons. I define a function *consumer* in Eq. 3.16.

$$consumer : hu_i^1 \mapsto \varnothing \qquad (3.16)$$

3.2.2 Simulation of EPCglobal Networks

After having defined formal entities to get a common sense of involved data entities in RFID-aided supply chains, I deal with the simulation of realistic event data for EPCglobal networks in the following. Real event data of industry-wide EPCglobal networks is not available due to privacy concerns and limited technology adoption. Nonetheless, event data are required to evaluate real-world characteristics of my proposed security extension. I have developed a discrete simulation model for event data as extension of the network simulator ns-3 [30]. The ns-3 simulator was originally developed for simulation of packet flows in communication networks.

Mapping: EPCglobal networks have a set of entities in common with communication networks. I define the mapping depicted in Fig. 3.3 for mapping of entities from either worlds to its corresponding abstraction as defined in Appendix A.2 in Table A.8. From the supply chain's perspective, I focus on the entities' participant, goods receiving, goods shipping area, transportation route, and freight vehicle.

Entities: For example, a supply chain participant is considered as the abstract entity node. Its equivalent entity in the ns-3 world is a concrete object of the class ns3::Node, e.g. a router or a switch in a communication network.

Node: Node refers to network nodes, such as routers, access points, bridges, etc., in ns-3 communication models [30]. In EPCglobal networks, nodes refer to individual supply chain participants as depicted in Fig. 1.1. I focus on the roles manufacturer, wholesaler, and retailer as defined by the formal model in Sect. 3.2.1. Each supply chain role is characterized by its position within the supply chain and the number of incoming and outgoing links. For instance, manufacturers are characterized by their first position within the supply chain, i.e. they have only outgoing links. Wholesalers have both in- and outgoing links. Retailers are located at the last position within the supply chain, i.e. they have only incoming links. Each supply chain participant performs internal processing steps with respect to its specific supply chain role.

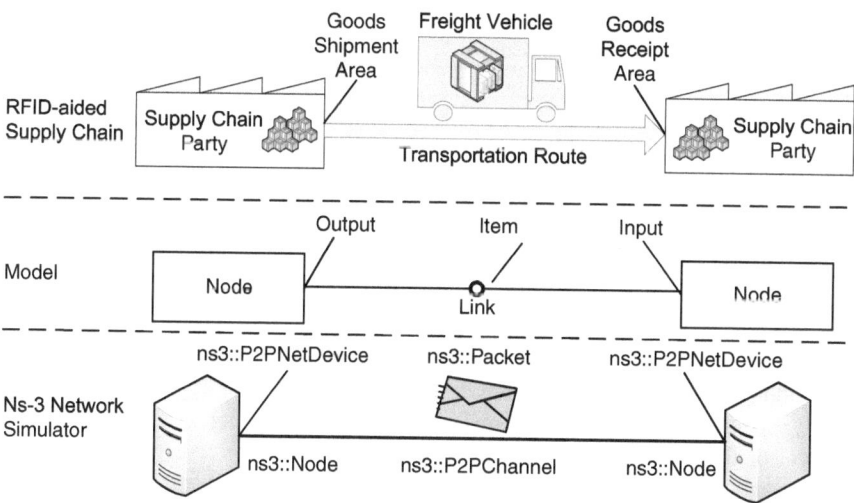

Fig. 3.3 Comparison of EPCglobal network and network simulator entities. For discrete event simulation entities of RFID-aided supply chains are mapped to network simulator entities

In-/Output: In-/Output locations of ns-3 nodes are not explicitly modeled. They belong to a `ns3::P2PNetDevice`, which are connected to network nodes. For fitting the requirements of EPCglobal networks, the class `ns3::P2PNetDevice` was extended by processing capabilities for in- and output locations.

Links: Links between communication nodes are implemented as `ns3::P2PChannel` in ns-3. They are connected to two objects of the class `ns3::NetDevice`. In EPCglobal networks links correspond to transportation routes on which goods are exchanged between participants by logistics provider.

Entity Handling Unit: Entity handling units define concrete packets that transmit data from one node to another via objects of the class `ns3::P2PChannel` in context of communication networks. Following the formal model for RFID-aided supply chains, packets refer to entity handling units of degree $k = 5$ for freight vehicles, such as aircrafts, ships, trucks, etc., which perform the transfer of goods [31]. Due to the fact that boxing and unboxing operations occur in EPC-global networks, I extended ns-3 by the container concept for k. A single container, pallet, etc. is an abstraction for a number of individual goods, which are shipped together.

Process Steps: The mapping of real-life business process steps to the simulation model involves an abstraction. I focused only on business processes that are recorded in EPCglobal networks as given in Table 3.3. Performed process steps depend on the concrete supply chain role, i.e. manufacturers do not perform `receiving` and `unpacking` while retailers do not perform `packing` and `shipping`. In context of the pharmaceutical supply chain, medicines are produced, packed to containers, and regularly shipped to wholesalers. After containers

Table 3.3 Mapping of business process steps and supply chain roles

Role	Receiving	Unpacking	Processing	Packing	Shipping
A			✔	✔	✔
B	✔	✔	✔	✔	✔
E	✔	✔	✔		

A = Manufacturer, B = Wholesaler, E = Retailer

have been received, they are unloaded, unpacked, processed, packed, and finally sent to the next participant in the supply chain. Additionally, observation events are recorded and stored in the company's EPCIS repository.

An excerpt of an EPCglobal network modeled as FMC petri net and the corresponding ns-nam visualization are depicted in Fig. 3.4. For approximation of the reality, specific supply chain parameters are configurable, e.g. container shipment interval or the variance of good processing time.

Receiving and Unpacking of Goods
Receiving goods is triggered by network mechanisms provided by ns-3. Incoming containers are unpacked to handle individual goods. Due to missing packing and unpacking functionality in ns-3, I implemented the class ns3::Container using a composite design pattern, i.e. a container object may subsume $0..n$ containers [32]. Containers can be used to define any entity degree while $k = 4$ is the default value.

Packing and Shipping of Goods
Goods are grouped as containers with respect to the link ratio specified by the supply chain model. The distribution of goods is determined by keeping statistics about the quantity of sent goods. The distribution algorithm evaluates the current ratio and analyzes the amount of goods sent during the last delivery with the amount of historically sent goods. Once certain shipping criteria are met, the filled container is shipped by invoking the ns-3 function ns3::Node::Send().

Generation of Realistic Event Data
The path of goods through the supply chain is tracked at every supply chain participant site. This is the basis for generation of realistic EPCglobal event data. Once a product passes one of the aforementioned process steps, a corresponding object event is generated, which conforms to EPCglobal standards [10]. Participant-specific data are randomly initialized during the setup phase of the simulation. In other words, Serial Shipping Container Code (SSCC), Serialized Global Trade Item Number (SGTIN), and Serialized Global Location Number (SGLN) are randomly attributed to provide a more realistic data distribution. However, the supply chain model is applied to all items individually. For example, subsequent packages passing the same location result in event data with identical SGLN.

In addition to object events, observe events are implemented, which are randomly triggered between distinct process steps. Its execution intervals are not

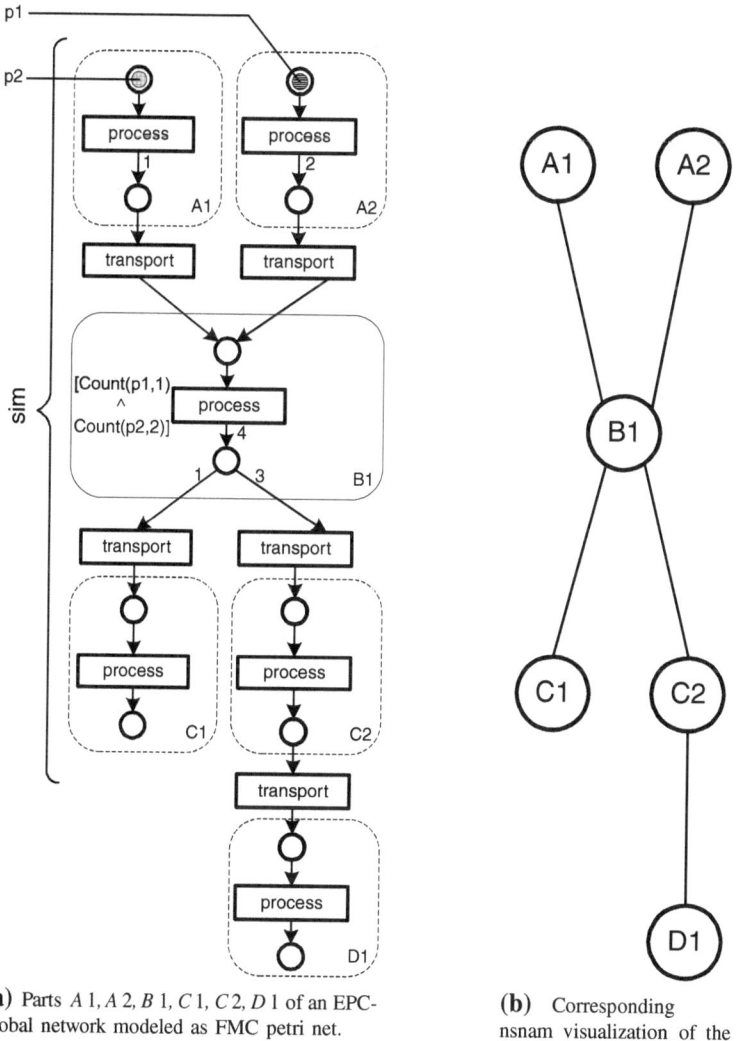

(**a**) Parts $A1, A2, B1, C1, C2, D1$ of an EPC-global network modeled as FMC petri net.

(**b**)   Corresponding nsnam visualization of the EPCglobal network.

Fig. 3.4 Comparison of **a** EPCglobal network petri net and **b** its corresponding ns-nam visualization

predefined, i.e. they occur at random times in the time interval between two process steps I value a random distribution of observe events as a realistic behavior, e.g. when a product is moved to the next available manufacturing area or prepared for an individual manufacturing step.

For further details regarding the simulation of EPCglobal network, please refer to existing literature [33].

3.3 Levels of Security

Having attained a common understanding of the aspects involved when discussing security in context of EPCglobal networks, I distinguish security aspects with respect to the relevant components and their primary location. Table 3.4 defines a *security matrix*, which classifies security in device-level and business-level and also considers the technical and the business view. This classification is used to distinguish individual security threats and countermeasures accordingly.

From the technical view, attackers may attempt to access device data, e.g. the EPC, but also information on the business level, such as data for goods receipt stored in an ERP system. From the business view, attackers can try to disrupt the relationship between devices and actual products on the device level or try to obtain details about suppliers or product owners on the business level. In the following, the classification in device- and business-level security is described in more detail.

3.3.1 Device-Level Security

I define *device-level security* as the sum of all efforts that aim to protect involved electronic equipment from malicious access, attacks or manipulation. In context of EPCglobal networks and RFID-aided supply chains, I refer to device as tags, readers, and all involved server systems, such as EPCIS repositories and ONS. In contrast to securing server systems, which is well understood in security engineering, protecting tags and readers need to be considered separately. Following the classification of security risks by Garfinkel et al. introduced in Sect. 2.1, I subdivide device-level security in security for devices (a) inside the supply chain and (b) within the transition zone [9]. Device-level security outside the supply chain remains out of focus of this work, as in this case the product has already left the supply chain in this case and cannot be controlled.

Device-Level Security Inside the Supply Chain
I refer to device-level security inside the supply chain, as all involved devices are solely controlled by supply chain participants. For instance, reader gates for RFID tags are installed at fixed locations therefore fully controlled by certain supply chain participants, e.g. a concrete wholesaler. From a security's point of view, these infrastructure components are located on the territory of the supply chain participant. I consider supply chain participants as interested in securing the

Table 3.4 Security matrix for EPCglobal networks. It classifies involved components as device or business level and introduces corresponding views

	Technical view	Business view
Device level	Tags, reader, hardware, etc.	Counterfeits
Business level	Sensitive business data	Business secrets

integrity of their own supply chain. I assume these devices physically secured comparable to other company equipment, e.g. by fences or gates.

Device-Level Security Within the Transition Zone

When referring to device-level security within the transition zone, I consider all involved devices that can move from inside to outside the supply chain. Therefore, these devices are not installed at fixed locations and they move through vulnerable environments that are not controlled by supply chain participants only. As a result, devices within the transition zone are exposed to malicious third parties when passing from one to another participant of the supply chain. For example, goods are equipped with RFID tags that move through the supply chain. In contrast to fixed installed reader gates, tempering with RFID tags is possible while shipping the linked goods. Due to the required transportation of goods, this security threat cannot be eliminated. Reducing time of unobserved transportation can improve product security since times without observation can be used by attackers to obtain the tag's content.

For example, increasing the amount of reading gates goods have to pass on their way through the supply chain or shielding tags from being read within the transition zone can improve tag protection. A possible implementation for the latter is known as the blocker tag, i.e. a dedicated supervising device escorting cargos equipped with tags, or the use of a Faraday cage, which shields any electromagnetic radiation [34]. Furthermore, software mechanisms can support protection of tags. For example, authentication mechanisms can prevent unauthorized access to tag data. From my perspective, the use of authentication mechanisms is promising for real-world scenarios since they can be applied to low-costs that are used for tracking and tracing scenarios nowadays. For further details about authentication protocols, please refer to Chap. 4.

3.3.2 Business-Level Security

In the following, I refer to *business-level security* in context of EPCglobal networks as all efforts that aim to protect sensitive business data from access by unauthorized third parties. This subsumes all existing activities to prevent access to enterprise systems. Due to the work's topic, I focus on business-relevant systems of EPCglobal networks only.

RFID Middleware

All captured events pass the middleware before reaching the EPCIS repository. From an enterprise application's point of view, the middleware acts as an internal user. Thus, user authentication and access control for the enterprise application is performed by the enterprise systems itself on the business level. Once an attacker controls the middleware system, it can be misused to inject malicious event data into the EPCIS repository. Authentication needs to be performed by the EPCIS repository when receiving new event data from the middleware system to protect the integrity of the stored event data.

EPCIS Repository

The EPCIS repository is a business-relevant system since it stores all event data related to goods movement at locations of involved supply chain roles A, B, C, E. From a security's point of view, the data flow of event data needs to be analyzed. It receives data from RFID middleware systems and RFID reader devices as introduced in Sect. 2.2. To prevent data manipulations, the EPCIS needs to be secured against any kind of third-party access with write capabilities. Reading event data can be performed either internally or externally. For example, internal business systems, such as ERP systems, access the EPCIS repository to update inventory details. Externally, anti-counterfeiting service providers require access to event data to verify the product's path within the supply chain.

Data protection of the EPCIS repository involves two aspects. Firstly, users need to be identified. This identification is the basis for granting access while being able to log user access. Secondly, specific data access needs to be granted only to authenticated users of the system. For authentication of users, an integration of existing enterprise authentication systems, such as Active Directory (AD) or Lightweight Directory Access Protocol (LDAP), is applicable. Granting access to event data is not straightforward. For example, the combination of event data can be misused to derive business knowledge. As a result, there is the requirement to control access to (a) event data as an atomic level of information and to (b) knowledge that can be derived by combining gathered event data.

The first can be achieved by applying existing access control mechanisms, such as RBAC as introduced in Sect. 2.1. The latter requires the analysis of data already exposed to a certain user. This is the motivation for HBAC described in more detail in Chap. 5.

3.4 In-Memory Technology Building Blocks

In the following section, I introduce selected in-memory technology building blocks that are incorporated into my developed security extensions. I refer to in-memory technology as a toolbox of technology artifacts to enable processing of enterprise data in real-time in the main memory. This includes the processing of hundreds of thousands of queries in a multi-user system in sub-second response time. In-memory technology enables decision taking in an interactive way without keeping redundant or pre-aggregated data.

Combined Column and Row Store: To support analytical and transactional operations, two optimized types of database systems have evolved. On the one hand, database systems for transactional workloads store and process data in a row-oriented format, i.e. attributes are stored side by side. On the other hand, database systems optimized for analytical purposes scan selected attributes of huge datasets in a very short time, e.g. by maintaining pre-aggregated totals. If complete data of a single row needs to be accessed, storing data in a row format is advantageous. For example, the comparison of two customers involves all of their database attributes, such as inquirers name, time, and content need to be loaded. In contrast, columnar stores benefit from their storage format, when only a subset of attributes needs to be processed. For example, summing up the total amount of products passed a certain reader gate involves the attributes date and business location, but the attributes EPC and business step are ignored. Using a row store for this purpose would result in processing of all attributes of the entire event list, although only two of these attributes are required. Therefore, a columnar store benefits from accessing only relevant data.

Insert-Only: Insert-only or append-only describes how new data are managed. Traditional database systems support four operations for data manipulations, i.e. insert, select, delete, and update of data. The latter two are considered to be destructive operations since original data are no longer available after its execution [35, Sect. 7.1]. In other words, it is neither possible to detect nor to reconstruct the complete history of values for a certain attribute after its execution since only the latest value is permanently stored. Insert-only tables enable storing the complete history of value changes and the latest value for a certain attribute [36]. For instance, this is the foundation of all bookkeeping systems to guarantee transparency. Insert-only builds the basis of storing the entire history of queries for access decisions of HBAC. In addition, insert-only enables tracing of access decisions, e.g. to perform incident analysis.

Lightweight Compression: *Compression* in context of in-memory technology refers to a mapping that defines a storage representation, which consumes less space than the original representation [36]. A columnar storage supports the use of lightweight compression techniques, such as run-length encoding, dictionary encoding, and differencing [37]. Due to the fixed data type per column, subsequent values are within a given interval, e.g. integer values. In addition, the given data type defines an upper threshold for individual values. Depending on the source of data, the number of concrete values is lower than all possible values from this interval, i.e. the amount of distinct values is required to store all data. This data representation requires only the amount of distinct values to store. For example, all incoming queries are stored in a log database table of the HBAC for analysis. If ten supply chain participants query details for the same product, it results in ten-times the same query. Instead of storing the query redundantly, dictionary compression stores the query once and maps it to a smaller integer representation. Within the database only the query's corresponding integer value is stored and database queries are rewritten to use the integer representation instead. The original representation is replaced just before the result set is returned to the client. As a result, the database executes all operations on compressed data without decompression. In comparison to the uncompressed format, which requires transferring ten-times the complete query string through the memory hierarchy of database server, the compressed data improves cache-hit ratio since more compressed data fits into the cache memory.

Partitioning: I distinguish the partitioning approaches vertical and horizontal partitioning [38]. *Vertical partitioning* refers to rearranging individual database columns. It is achieved by splitting columns of a database table in two or more sets of columns. Each of the sets can be distributed on individual databases servers. This technique can also be used to build up database columns with different ordering to achieve better search performance while guaranteeing high-availability of data [39]. Key to success of vertical partitioning is a thorough understanding of data access patterns. Attributes that are accessed in the same query should rely in the same partition since locating and joining additional columns result in degradation of overall performance.

In contrast, *horizontal partitioning* addresses long database tables and their division into smaller chunks of data. As a result, each portion of the database table contains a subset of the complete data. Splitting data in equivalent long horizontal partitions is used to support parallel search operations and to improve scalability. For example, a scan of the complete query history results in a full table scan. With a single partition, a single thread needs to access all individual history entries to check the relevant predicate for selection. When using a nave round robin horizontal partitioning across ten partitions, the scan of the complete table is performed in parallel by ten threads simultaneously. It reduces the response time by approx. one ninth compared to the aforementioned single threaded approach.

This example shows that the partition length depends on the incorporated partitioning strategy. For example, instead of using round robin, range partitioning can be used, e.g. inquirers are portioned in groups of 1,000 with the help of their user id or requested EPC.

Multi-Core and Parallelization: Parallelization can be applied to various locations within the application stack of enterprise systems—from within the application running on an application server to query execution in the database system. As an example of application-level parallelism, I assume the following. Incoming queries need to be processed in parallel by EPCIS repositories to satisfy response time expectations. Processing multiple queries can be handled by multi-threaded applications, i.e. the application does not stall when dealing with more than one query at a time. Operating systems threads are a software abstraction that needs to be mapped to physically available hardware resources [40, Chap. 2]. A CPU core is comparable to a single worker on a construction area. If it is possible to map each query to a single core, the systems response time is optimal. Query processing also involves data processing, i.e. the database needs to be queried in parallel, too. If the database is able to distribute the workload across multiple cores a single server works optimal. If the workload exceeds physical capacities of a single system, multiple servers or blades need to be installed for distribution of work to achieve optimal processing behavior. From the database point of view, data partitioning supports parallelization since multiple CPU cores even on multiple servers can process data simultaneously [41, Chap. 6]. This example shows that multi-core architectures and parallelization depend on each other while partitioning is the basis for parallel data processing.

Active and Passive Data Store: I define two categories of data stores: *active* and *passive*. I refer to active data when it is accessed frequently and regular updates are expected, e.g. access rules of HBAC. In contrast, passive data are neither updated nor accessed regularly. They are purely used for analytical and statistical purposes or in exceptional situations where specific investigations require these data. For example, tracking events of a certain pharmaceutical product that was sold five years ago can be considered as passive data. Firstly, from the business' perspective, the pharmaceutical can be consumed until the best-before date of two years after its manufacturing date has been reached. When the product is handled now, five years after its manufacturing, it is no longer permitted to be sold. Secondly, the product was most probably sold to a customer four years ago, i.e. it left the supply chain and is typically already used within its best-before data. Therefore, the probability that details about this pharmaceutical are queried is very low. Nonetheless, the tracking history is conserved and no data is deleted in conformance to legal regulations. As a result, the passive data can still be accessed but with a higher latency than active data. For example, passive data can be used for reconstructing the path of a product within the supply chain or for financial long-term forecast. This example gives an understanding of active and passive data. Furthermore, introducing the concept of passive data result in a classification of data stores. Thus, active data that need to be accessed in real-time can be separated from passive data that is ready for archiving.

When data are moved to a passive data store they no longer consume fast accessible main memory. Dealing with passive data stores involves the definition of a memory hierarchy including fast, but expensive, and slow, but cheap memory. A possible storage hierarchy is given by: memory registers, cache memory, main memory, flash storages, solid state disks, SAS hard disk drives, SATA hard disk drives, tapes, etc. To distinguish between active and passive data, rules for migration of data from one store to another needs to be defined. I refer to them as *data aging strategy* or *aging rules*. I consider the process of aging, i.e. the migration of data from a fast to a slower store as background task, which is performed regularly, e.g. once a month or once a week. Since this process involves reorganization of the entire database, it should be performed only during times of low database access, e.g. during nights or weekends.

Reduction of Layers: In application development, layers refer to levels of abstraction. Each application layer encapsulates specific logic and offers certain functionality. Although abstraction helps to reduce complexity, it also introduces obstacles. Examples for the latter are (a) functionality is hidden within a layer and (b) each layer offers a variety of functionalities while only a small subset is in use. From the data point of view, layers are problematic since data are marshaled and un-marshaled for transformation to the layer-specific format. As a result, identical data are present in various layers and representations. A reduction of layer improves the use of hardware resources. Moving application logic to the data it operates on results in a smaller application stack and also code reduction. Reducing the code length results in improved maintainability.

HBAC is implemented as a single layer application in Python and interacts directly with the in-memory database. As a result, processing overhead due to multiple layers is already addressed by its design.

References

1. Office of Transportation and Machinery U.S. Department of Commerce. U.S. Automotive Parts Industry Annual Assessment (2011), http://trade.gov/wcm/groups/public/@trade/@mas/@man/@aai/documents/web_content/auto_reports_parts2009.pdf. Accessed 8 Mar 2012
2. International Organization for Standardization. ISO/IEC 9001:2008—Quality Management Systems—Requirements, (2008)
3. International Organization for Standardization. Expected outcomes for accredited certification to ISO 9001 (2011), http://www.iso.org/iso/definitive_expected_outcomes_iso9001.pdf. Accessed 8 Mar 2012
4. Federal Office for Information Security. BSI Standard 100–1: Information Security Management, System V.1.5 (2008)
5. International Organization for Standardization. ISO/IEC 27001:2005—Information Technology—Security Techniques—Information Security Management Systems–Requirements (2005)
6. S. Wendt, *Nichtphysikalische Grundlagen der Informationstechnik: Interpretierte Formalismen*, Vol 2 (Springer, Berlin, 1991)
7. M. Stamp, *Information Security: Principles and Practice*. (John Wiley and Sons, New York, 2006)
8. Federal Office for Information Security. BSI Standard 100–3: Risk Analysis based on IT-Grundschutz V. 2.5 (2008)
9. Simson L. Garfinkel, Ari Juels, Ravi Pappu, RFID privacy: an overview of problems and proposed solutions. IEEE Secur. Priv. **3**, 34–43 (2005)
10. Global Standards 1. Tag Data Standards 1.6 (2011), http://www.gs1.org/gsmp/kc/epcglobal/tds/tds_1_6-RatifiedStd-20110922.pdf. Accessed 8 Mar 2012
11. M-P. Schapranow, A. Zeier, F. Leupold, T. Schubotz, Securing EPCglobal Object Name Service—Privacy Enhancements for Anti-counterfeiting. In *Proceedings of the 2nd International Conference on Intelligent Systems, Modeling and Simulation*. IEEE Computer Society, (2011), pp. 332–337
12. M-P. Schapranow, A. Zeier, H. Plattner, A Dynamic Mutual RFID Authentication Model Preventing Unauthorized Third Party Access. In *Proceedings of the 4th International Conference on Network and System Security*, (2010)
13. K. Koscher et al., EPC RFID Tags in Security Applications: Passport Cards, Enhanced Drivers Licenses, and Beyond. Manuscript (2008)
14. H. Hwang et al., A Study on MITM Vulnerability in Wireless Network Using 802.1X and EAP. In *Proceedings of the International Conference on Information Science and Security*, Washington, DC, USA, IEEE Computer Society, (2008), pp. 164–170
15. Global Standards 1. EPC Radio-Frequency Identity Protocols - Class-1 Generation-2 UHF RFID Protocol for Communications at 860 MHz - 960 MHz - 1.2.0 (2008), http://www.gs1.org/gsmp/kc/epcglobal/uhfc1g2/uhfc1g2_1_2_0-standard-20080511.pdf. Accessed 8 Mar 2012
16. Hossein Bidgoli, *Handbook of Information Security* (John Wiley and Sons, Inc., New York, 2006)
17. Bayer Technology Services. Sicher, schnell & einfach - Einmalige Zufallszahlen mit dem BayCoder (2011), http://www.bayertechnology.com/uploads/media/Infoblatt_TTA_BayCoder_D_030811.pdf. Accessed 8 Mar 2012

18. J.M. Stewart, E. Tittel, M. Chapple, *Certified Information Systems Security Professional Study Guide*, 3rd edn. (Sybex, New York, 2005)
19. D. Russell, G.T. Gangemi, Sr. *Computer Security Basics* (O'Reilly & Associates Inc., Sebastopol, 1991)
20. A. Juels, *Minimalist Cryptography for Low-Cost RFID Tags*, eds. by C. Blundo, S. Cimato Security in Communication Networks. Lecture Notes in Computer Science, Vol 3352 (Springer, Berlin , 2005), pp. 149–164
21. M. Beck, E. Tews, Practical Attacks against WEP and WPA (2008), http://dl.aircrack-ng.org/breakingwepandwpa.pdf. Accessed 8 Mar 2012
22. W. Stallings, *Cryptography and Network Security*, 4th edn. (Prentice Hall, New Delh, 2005)
23. U. Waldmann, U. Waldmann, K. Sohr, *RFID-Studie 2007: Technologieintegrierte Datensicherheit bei RFID-Systemen* (Studie, Fraunhofer-Institut für Sichere Informations-Technologie (SIT), Darmstadt, 2007)
24. I. Sommerville, *Software Engineering*. (Addison-Wesley, New York, 2007)
25. Supply Chain Council. Supply Chain Operations Reference Model V.10. Whitepaper (2010)
26. M-P. Schapranow et al., *What are Authentic Pharmaceuticals Worth?*, chapter 13 (INTECH Press, New York, 2011), pp. 203–220
27. L. Vilkov, B. Weiß, *Prozessorientierte Wirtschaftlichkeitsanalyse von RFID-Systemen anhand eines Referenz-Wirkungsmodells* (Springer, Heidelberg, 2008), pp. 275–304
28. G.F. Knolmayer, P. Mertens, A. Zeier, *Supply Chain Management Based on SAP Systems: Architecture and Planning Processes* SAP Excellence (Springer, Berlin, 2009)
29. J. Müller et al., RFID Middleware as a Service—Enabling Small and Medium-sized Enterprises to Participate in the EPC Network. In *Proceedings of the 16th International Conference on Industry Engineering and Engineering Management*, Vol 2 (2009), pp. 2040–2043
30. T.R. Henderson et al., Network Simulations with the ns-3 Simulator. *Computer Engineering* (2006), pp. 173-182
31. M-P. Schapranow, A. Zeier, H. Plattner, A Formal Model for Enabling RFID in Pharmaceutical Supply Chains. In *Proceedings of the 44th Hawaii International Conference on System Sciences* (2011)
32. E. Gamma, *Design Patterns: Elements of Reusable Object-oriented Software* (Addison-Wesley, London, 1995)
33. M-P. Schapranow, C. Faehnrich, A. Zeier, H. Plattner, Simulation of RFID-aided Supply Chains: Case Study of the Pharmaceutical Industry. In *Proceedings of the 3rd International Conference on Computational Intelligence, Modelling and, Simulation*, (2011)
34. A. Juels, R.L. Rivest, M. Szydlo, The Blocker Tag: Selective Blocking of RFID Tags for Consumer Privacy. In *Proceedings of the 10th Conference on Computer and Communication Security*, New York, NY, USA, (2003), pp. 103–111
35. M-P. Schapranow, Transaction Processing 2.0: The Epochal Change in Designing Transaction Processing Systems. Master's thesis, Hasso Plattner Institute (2008)
36. H. Plattner, A. Zeier, *In-Memory Data Management: An Inflection Point for Enterprise Applications* (Springer, Berlin, 2011)
37. P. Svensson, The Evolution of Vertical Database Architectures—A Historical Review. In *Proceedings of the 20th International Conference on Scientific and Statistical Database Management* (Springer, New York, 2008), pp. 3–5
38. S. Lightstone, T.J. Teorey, T. Nadeau, *Physical Database Design: The Database Professional's Guide to Exploiting Indexes, Views, Storage, and more* (Elsevier, New York, 2007)
39. J.M. Hellerstein, M. Stonebraker, J. Hamilton, *Architecture of a Database System, Foundation and Trends in Databases*, Vol 1 (Now Publishers, New York, 2007)
40. S. Andrew, *Tanenbaum Modern Operating Systems*, 3rd edn. (Prentice Hall Press, Paramus, 2008)
41. J.M. Hellerstein, M. Stonebraker, *Readings in Database Systems*, 4th edn. (MIT Press, New York, 2005)

Chapter 4
Device-Level Extensions

In the preceding chapter, I depicted possible attacks that motivate the need for specific security requirements for RFID environments. The following chapter deals with concrete device-level security extensions for use in combination with low-cost RFID tags to keep product surcharges low. To support the fast adoption of RFID technology in the pharmaceutical supply chain, I developed the following authentication protocols to address device-level security aspects. They are designed to keep tag production costs low due to my assumption that this is the primary barrier for wide spreading of RFID-aided supply chains and EPCglobal networks in the pharmaceutical supply chain. In terms of the security matrix introduced in Sect. 3.3 device-level security extensions focus on (a) tag and reader devices from the technical view and (b) product counterfeits from the business view. In the following, I introduce authentication protocols, which were designed for use with passive low-cost tags from the technical perspective while improving the detection of product counterfeits from the business perspective.

Authentication: *Authentication* in terms of EPCglobal networks describes the process of confirming the identity of communication partners [1]. An authentication protocol has to ensure a high level of data integrity to be a promising candidate for implementation within the pharmaceutical supply chain as introduced in Sect. 1.1. On the one hand, RFID tags are placed in vulnerable environments where it is not possible to guarantee the authenticity of any reader. On the other hand, the reader device is also not able to guarantee that a certain tag is the desired communication partner. Related work showed that current research activities in the field of security in RFID-aided supply chains focuses on preventing security threats individually as introduced in Sect. 3.1. In other words, a dedicated solution is implemented to address a specific security threat in a special context instead of preventing multiple security threats by a single solution. This results in raised chip-level complexity and increased tag production costs when data security is improved. Available on-tag resources of passive low-cost tags are very limited compared to current portable computers or modern cellular phones. In other words, keeping resource demands low for authentication protocols results in minimized and stable tag production costs.

Matthieu-P. Schapranow, *Real-time Security Extensions for EPCglobal Networks*,
In-Memory Data Management Research, DOI: 10.1007/978-3-642-36343-6_4,
© Springer-Verlag Berlin Heidelberg 2014

I discuss mutual authentication protocols in the following to understand their benefits and challenges. *Mutual authentication* refers to the fact that both communication peers can trust the other communication peers' authenticity [2]. For instance, a trusted third party that can be queried by peers to testify their relationship can verify the authenticity of communication partners. The use of mutual authentication protocols is promising for the industry, because implementations build on the use of low-cost tags while addressing a multifarious number of security threats. The developed mutual authentication protocols are applicable for fast-moving goods, which is a requirement for the pharmaceutical industry. From the customer's point of view, these protocols establish a reliable level of privacy, because they do not expose any product details after buying a product, e.g. when leaving the pharmacy with a package of medicines. In contrast to existing solutions addressing the privacy aspect, the presented protocols do not need to destroy tags permanently to reliably control access to on-tag data [3].

Requirements: The given mutual authentication protocols were designed with the following requirements in mind:

- Clear-text communication between tag and reader must not be interpretable by unauthorized third parties,
- Tags must not communicate with unauthorized reader devices, and
- Readers must not communicate with unauthorized tags.

The static mutual authentication protocol described in Sect. 4.1 stores a predefined list of passwords on the tag. This protocol is designed for supply chains with a known limited number of participants to prevent reuse of stolen tags and tag cloning. The second approach introduced in Sect. 4.2 is more flexible with respect to the supply chain layout. It builds on passwords stored on the tag, which are dynamically updated after each successful communication. Both approaches use non-cryptic hash functions, such as Fowler-Noll-Vo, Jenkins, or Zobrist, to impede unwanted tag reading with commodity reader hardware.

4.1 Static List Low-Cost Mutual Authentication Protocol

Implementing authentication results in an extension of the existing communication protocol between reader and tag. The UML sequence diagram given in Fig. 4.1 depicts the extended communication protocol of the low-cost mutual authentication protocol. The setup follows the concept of PKIs with a trusted third party [4, Chap. 13]. In addition to tag and reader, an authentication database is depicted, which contains details for authentication of tags and readers.

Authentication Process: The authentication process involves the following process steps.

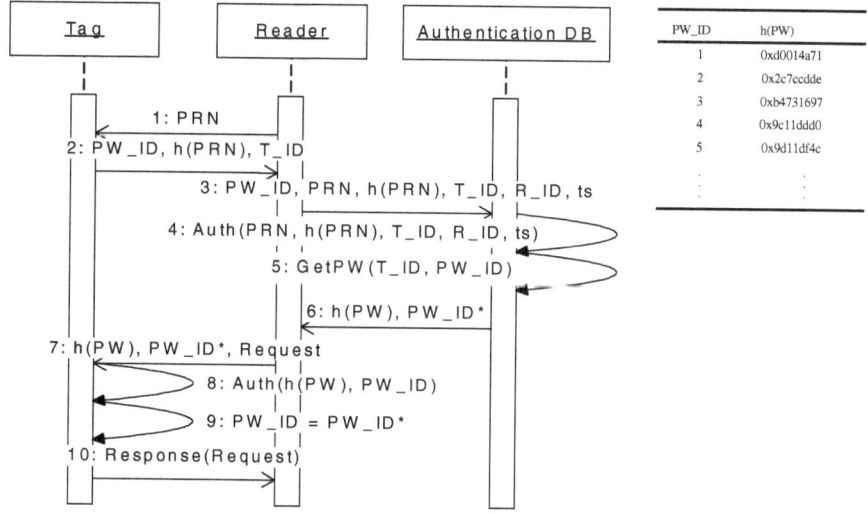

Fig. 4.1 UML sequence diagram depicting enhanced communication protocol of the static list low-cost mutual authentication protocol involving the authentication database as trusted third party for tags and readers. On the *top right*, a static on-tag password list is exemplarily depicted. PW_ID defines the index of the *hashed* password h(PW)

1. The reader initiates the communication with the tag by sending a Pseudo Random Number (PRN). Instead of generating each time a new PRN, it is generated once a minute and is used for all queries performed by the reader within the next minute. This reduces the performance impact of generating an excessive amount of unique PRNs within a short period of time, e.g. when hundreds of tags are processed per minute. The algorithm for generating PRNs is reader-specific, i.e. each reader performs a generic algorithm with a specific offset to generate unique PRNs [5].

2. The tag receives the PRN and performs a one-way hash function on it. The hash function uses tag-specific parameters to create an individual offset. The latter were persisted during the manufacturing process of the tag to create an offset for the used hash function, e.g. the variation of the initial SRAM state on the tag [6]. The generated hashed PRN h(PRN) is sent with a random password identifier PW_ID and a tag-specific tag identifier T_ID back to the reader. The tag contains a unique password list, which is valid during its lifetime. The list was initiated by the authentication database and contains shared secrets. The PW_ID is used to reference a specific password from this list. The tag expects the reader to send the indicated password within the next message. The correct password authenticates the reader.

3. The reader enriches the received triple by its initially generated PRN, the timestamp ts describing the point in time when PRN was generated, and its identifier R_ID. This information is used to authenticate the reader device against the authentication database. The tuple is passed to the authentication database to perform the authentication step Auth().

4. The authentication database contains sensitive data about the specific hash offsets, i.e. the offset for the tag-specific hash function and the offset used by the reader to generate PRNs. Both parties have to trust this single source of truth. To validate the received tuple the following steps are performed:

   - Lookup the received R_ID and perform network checks, e.g. to validate whether the request was received through a trusted network connection via a valid route registered for the specified reader,
   - Check whether the generated PRN is valid for the given R_ID in the given ts, i.e. apply the reader algorithm stored in the database to generate the PRN. If the generated PRN matches with the received one, the reader is authenticated against the authentication database, and
   - Perform the tag-specific hash function h for the identified tag T_ID with the given PRN. If the outcome matches with the given h(PRN) the tag is authenticated against the authentication database.

5. The authentication database retrieves PW identified by PW_ID from its secure store. It performs the tag-specific hash function to generate h(PW). Both, h(PW) and the next password identifier PW_ID* are sent to the reader.

6. The reader forwards the tuple consisting of h(PW) and PW_ID* to the tag. The Request for the tag content is piggybacked.

7. The tag receives the tuple consisting of h(PW), PW_ID*, and Request.

8. The tag authenticates the reader in the following way:

   - Lookup the tag's password list to identify the current PW and calculate its hash value h(PW), and
   - Compare the received h(PW) with the locally generated. Since the reader receives the valid h(PW) only after successful authentication, the tag can assume a validated reader device since the correct h(PW) was provided.

9. The tag invalidates the locally stored password for the entry PW_ID and replaces the current password identifier by PW_ID*.

10. The Response(Request) for the Request is sent back to the reader.

4.2 Space-Aware Mutual Authentication Protocol

In the following, I introduce the space-aware mutual authentication protocol as depicted in Fig. 4.2. In contrast to the static mutual authentication protocol introduced in Sect. 4.1 the dynamic one does not rely on the concrete supply chain layout.

Dynamic refers to password generation following the principle of OTPs and its exchange using hash functions with tag-specific offsets. A randomized password and a parameterized hash function offset, which is determined by the current

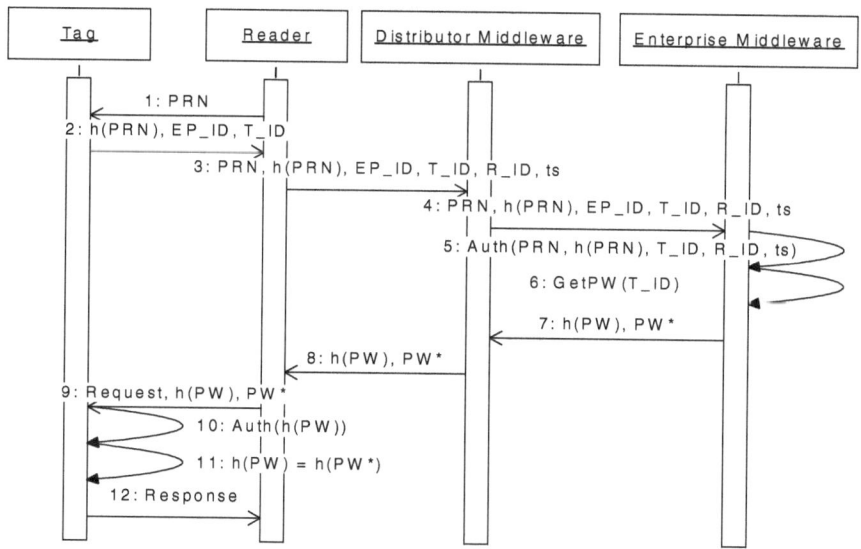

Fig. 4.2 UML sequence diagram depicting the enhanced communication protocol for the space-aware mutual authentication protocol. The distributor middleware forwards gathered tag and reader details for authentication checking to the enterprise middleware that initialized the tag. In contrast to the static mutual authentication protocol, only a single *hashed* password, e.g. $h(PW) = 0xd0014a71$, is stored on the tag and replaced after each successful communication

password and the result of a Physical Uncloneable Function (PUF) are stored on the tag during its initialization phase [7]. The authentication protocol requires the calculation of hash values of updated passwords to replace existing ones. The hash function guarantees that no clear-text passwords are exchanged between reader and tag via the ether. The correct hash value is required for authorization of the reader. This authentication protocol is referred to as dynamic authentication since the password stored on the tag is updated after each successful authentication process. The tag-specific offset is a shared secret, known by the tag and the enterprise that initialized the tag, i.e. tags with write-once, read-many capabilities are required as described in Sect. 2.2.

The authentication protocol involves a distributor and an enterprise middleware. All reader devices are connected through the distributor middleware to the enterprise middleware. The latter contains details about all tags initialized by the enterprise. Every tag holds a specific enterprise identifier EP_ID and a tag identifier T_ID. EP_ID maps the tag to its enterprise and T_ID identifies it within the database of the enterprise middleware.

Authentication Process: Figure 4.2 depicts the dynamic mutual authentication protocol modeled as UML sequence diagram, which consists of the following steps.

1. The reader sends the PRN to the tag.
2. The tag's response consists of the hash value h(PRN), the tag identifier T_ID, and the enterprise identifier EP_ID.

3. The reader adds PRN, T_ID, and the active timestamp ts when PRN was generated to the received data. This tuple is forwarded to its connected distributor middleware.

4. The distributor middleware contacts the tag's enterprise identified by EP_ID. It sends PRN, h(PRN), T_ID, R_ID, and ts to the tag's enterprise middleware.

5. The enterprise middleware authenticates reader and tag by validating the generated PRN and the submitted hash value h(PRN).

6. If the enterprise middleware contains details about the tag specified by T_ID, the current password and the tag-specific offset for the hash function are retrieved to calculate the hash value of the current password.

7. If the tag is valid, the enterprise middleware generates the hash value h(PW) for the current password and returns a new password PW*. The PW* is forwarded to the tag to replace the stored password. The received h(PW) ensures the authenticity of the reader from the tag's perspective. The hashed password h(PW) and PW* are sent to the distributor middleware.

8. The distributor middleware receives the answer from the enterprise middleware and passes the data to the connected reader.

9. The authenticated reader sends the Request piggybacked with h(PW) and PW* to the reader.

10. The tag compares the received h(PW) with the stored hash value to verify the authenticity of the reader. If both values match, the reader is authorized to access data on the tag.

11. The tag creates a hash value of the received new password PW* and replaces the current h(PW) by it.

12. The tag responds to the Request and sends the Response back to the reader.

4.3 Security Evaluation

In the following, I evaluate the introduced mutual authentication protocols with respect to the security threats introduced in Sect. 3.1.2. I consider connections between middleware servers and readers as secure. Thus, I focus only on security threats concerning the communication between tags and readers.

Cloning and Spoofing Attacks
Traditional tags are vulnerable against cloning attacks, i.e. once an attacker is able to access the tag's content, a clone with identical content can be replicated multiple times. Low-cost tags are neither equipped with computational power nor contain enhanced security components as described in Sect. 2.2. Copying the complete content of the tag is the basis for product counterfeits. A counterfeit equipped with a cloned tag inherits the product history of its valid original

pendant. The design of the static authentication protocol limits the possibility of re-using cloned tags, because the tag stops working after a predefined number of queries when all passwords were invalidated.

Spoofing of RFID tags exploits a trusted relationship between two peers. Either cloning the original tag or deriving information about the content of a virtual non-existing tag can achieve this exploit.

The use of an authentication protocol strengthens tags against cloning and spoofing, because the tag-specific hash function has to be imitated by attackers. Although the hash function is a generic one, the tag-specific offset derived from material discrepancies makes its calculation results tag-specific and therefore harder to simulate. The introduced authentication protocols work without the need of any kind of on-tag PRN generator, which require more computational power than the incorporated hash function [8]. Spoofing a tag implies eavesdropping the communication between tag and reader in protocol steps one and two of individual authentication protocols or sending requests by an adversary reader itself. Storing the response of a certain tag for all possibly PRNs in a mapping table is necessary to generate the illusion of a perfectly spoofed tag. Such a faked tag is able to answer all reader requests in the same way as the original tag by looking up responses from its mapping table. An adversary has to follow the original tag to fill-up the complete mapping table of the spoofed tag. This is a time-consuming process depending on the input domain used for generation of PRNs.

Assuming physical and technical constraints, a reader processes about one hundred tag requests per second [9]. Acquiring all possible values of an eight-bit long PRN requires attacking the tag for about 2.5 s. Increasing the input domain of the PRN to 24 bits, results in about two days of attacks; with a 30-bit input domain of the PRN, attacks consume more than four months. I assume that the latter exceeds the product lifecycle of fast-moving goods in the pharmaceutical supply chain.

Only authentic tags are able to send valid combinations of the required hashed values, e.g. h(PRN) and tag-specific details. For instance, the static authentication protocol requires a valid T_ID while the dynamic authentication protocol requires a valid combination of EP_ID and T_ID. As a result, the following attack scenarios are possible.

- **T_ID**: If a tag sends an invalid T_ID it is detected by both authentication protocols. The static authentication protocol detects an invalid T_ID during the authentication in protocol step [four] performed by the authentication database. The hashed response is generated in this step using the T_ID to lookup the incorporated hash function offset, which results in a mismatch of h(PRN). In the dynamic authentication protocol an invalid T_ID is detected by the enterprise middleware during the authentication in protocol step [five] comparable to the static authentication protocol. Therefore, the tag is not identified as a part of the enterprise given by its EP_ID. The enterprise middleware informs the distributor middleware about this mismatch and the tag can be identified as unauthentic.

- **EP_ID**: The EP_ID is only used by the dynamic authentication protocol. When providing a faked EP_ID the distributor middleware cannot connect to the specific enterprise middleware in protocol step [four]. As a result, the tag can be identified as unauthentic.
- **h(PRN)**: If a random hash value is sent by the tag in response for the given PRN, the authentication database or enterprise middleware detects it comparable to an invalid T_ID during the authentication step.

Man-in-the-Middle Attacks

Both authentication protocols address MITM attacks by invalidating required password after a successful communication. The static authentication protocol benefits from the predefined password list. If the static on-tag password list is invalidated the lifecycle of the tag automatically ends, i.e. a kill password is not required. However, the static authentication protocol requires concrete knowledge of the supply chain layout to determine an appropriate length of the password list during tag initialization.

Although neither of both authentication protocols prevents third parties from eavesdropping the communication, they prevent MITM attacks. Since a single password can only be used once, eavesdroppers cannot re-use captured data for another tag or in combination with a replay attack. Once, the reader receives the proper hash value from the authentication database or enterprise middleware, the request is sent back to the tag and a new password updates the current one.

Replay Attacks

A replay attack in terms of the pharmaceutical supply chain can be implemented by acquiring the h(PW) for accessing the content of the tag. Replay attacks are addressed by the use of OTPs. A hashed password can only be used for a single communication between tag and reader. A gathered hashed password cannot be re-used for a replay attack. For example, an attacker repeats protocol step 9 to achieve a replay attack in context of the dynamic authentication protocol. The attacker requires a former h(PW). However, once h(PW) was used, it is automatically invalidated in protocol step 11.

For a concrete OTP implementation, it is crucial to consider a proper way of generating passwords to prevent brute-force guessing attacks [10]. Distributed Denial-of-Service (DDos) attacks reducing the service availability or for guessing of valid password are prevented by returning invalid responses. Once a predefined messages-per-second threshold is exceeded, the tag only returns a default message instead of the correct response. As a result, the required time for completing attacks increases.

Signal Interferences

Controlled signal interferences can shield reader messages from tags and vice versa regardless of the incorporated authentication protocol. Instead of receiving the intended original data, malicious requests can be issued this way. If an attacker is able to shield the tag from getting both, the reader's request and the captured hashed password during protocol step 7 of the static or during protocol step 9 of the dynamic protocol, the original request can be changed by the attacker. However, this attack can only be performed for a single tag and not for a series of tags. Furthermore, it requires accurate timing capabilities to shield messages for a specific tag. As a result, I consider controlled signal interferences as a very complex task in environments with hundreds or thousands of tags.

4.4 Summary

The outlined mutual authentication protocols extend the existing EPCglobal communication protocol by exchanging tag specific details. The use of OTPs prevents unknown third parties from accessing on-tag data. Hash functions are incorporated to prevent exchange of sensitive password in clear text. Required computational on-tag capabilities to calculate hash values is low in comparison to encryption/decryption functionality since only a subset of gate equivalents is required to implement hash functions [11]. Hash functions require extension of low-cost tags, but not necessarily the use of more expensive active tags. As a result, the expected manufacturing costs of the required tags are higher than for comparable passive low-cost tags but remain below costs for active tags. The authentication database of the static authentication protocol needs to be operated as a central instance by an independent third party. All supply chain participants need to trust this party. Thus, without knowing each participant in the supply chain, it enables trusted exchange of products in open supply chains. Installation and operating costs can be amortized through supply chain participants, e.g. by product surcharges. In contrast, the enterprise middleware of the dynamic authentication protocol needs to be operated by manufacturers, which initialize the tags. The connection between reader and authentication database can be implemented on top of existing communication networks such as the Internet. The communication can be secured by using SSL encryption based on X.509 certificates or VPNs.

Which of the presented authentication protocols is the adequate one for which purposes? The answer depends on the supply chain layout. In static supply chains with known read locations the static authentication protocol is preferable. The finite list of passwords makes it impossible to re-use a stolen tag in connection with counterfeits after all valid passwords were consumed. Due to the use of continuously updated OTPs the dynamic authentication protocol is preferable when the manufacturer does not know the complete supply chain layout at tag initialization time. Both authentication protocols have in common that they prevent unauthorized third parties to access the tag. They do not address eavesdropping of exchanged messages. But, they restrict the usage of eavesdropped messages for typical attacks, such as replay attacks.

References

1. D.-H. Seo, J.-M. Baek, D. Cho, Secure RFID authentication scheme for EPC class Gen2, in *Proceedings of the 3rd International Conference on Ubiquitous Information Management and Communication* (ACM, New York, 2009), pp. 221–227
2. D.C. Ranasimghe, Lightweight cryptography for low cost RFID, in *Networked RFID Systems and Lightweight Cryptography*, vol. 4. (Springer, 2008), pp. 311–346
3. Global standards 1: EPC radio-frequency identity protocols—class-1 generation-2 UHF RFID protocol for communications at 860 MHz–960 MHz - 1.2.0, (2008), http://www.gs1.org/gsmp/kc/epcglobal/uhfc1g2/uhfc1g2_1_2_0-standard-20080511.pdf. Accessed 8 Mar 2012
4. A.J. Menezes, S.A. Vanstone, P.C. Van Oorschot, *Handbook of Applied Cryptography* (CRC Press, Inc., Boca Raton, 1996)
5. A. Juels, Minimalist cryptography for low-cost RFID tags, in *Security in Communication Networks*, ed. by C. Blundo, S. Cimato. Lecture Notes in Computer Science, vol. 3352. (Springer, Berlin, 2005), pp. 149–164
6. D.E. Holcomb, W.P. Burleson, Initial SRAM state as a fingerprint and source of true random numbers for RFID tags, in *Proceedings of the Conference on RFID Security*, July, 2007
7. P. Tuyls, L. Batina, RFID-tags for anti-counterfeiting, in *Proceedings of the RSA Conference on Topics in Cryptology*. Lecture Notes in Computer Science, vol. 3860. (Springer, Heidelberg, 2006), pp. 115–131
8. B. Song, C.J. Mitchell, RFID authentication protocol for low-cost tags, in *Proceedings of the 1st Conference on Wireless Network Security* (ACM, New York, 2008), pp. 140–147
9. H. Birgit, RFID: technology, systems and applications, in *Federal Association for Information Technology Telecommunications and New Media*, Whitepaper, 2005
10. A.S. Tanenbaum, *Computer Networks*, 4th edn. (Prentice Hall, New Jersey, 2003)
11. M. Feldhofer, S. Dominikus, J. Wolkerstorfer, Strong authentication for RFID systems using the AES algorithm, in *Proceedings of the 6th International Workshop on Cryptographic Hardware and Embedded Systems*, pp. 357–370, 2004

Chapter 5
Business-Level Extensions for Event Repositories

In the following chapter, I introduce the developed transparent security extensions based on my implementation of HBAC. I refer to HBAC as all access control mechanisms that store a complete history of queries, analyze it, and perform decision taking based on its evaluations. My contribution is designed for extension of current EPCIS implementations. With respect to Hyp. 2 the following requirements are considered to control data access:

- **User Authentication:** Identify the inquirer and protocol, who is querying data from the EPCIS repository,
- **Access Rights:** Enforce, which portion of data is allowed to be accessed by whom, and
- **Secured Data Exchange:** Prevent manipulation of data during its exchange between client and EPCIS repository.

Application Example: From my perspective, combining event data with semantic information can lead to exposure of sensitive business secrets. Consider a pharmaceutical manufacturer and one of the competitors querying the EPCIS repository. The competitor sends a query for details of a guessed EPC of one product's ingredients. Even if the default access rule prohibits returning any details to unknown parties, the fact that an empty message instead of no message is returned indicates the existence of further data for the given EPC, which exposes the relationship with the supplier as defined by threat T2 in Sect. 3.1. In real life, none would provide supplier details to competitors. Let us assume further, the competitor continues to query details of a second, third, etc. supplier. The existence of further details in your EPCIS repository can be combined to derive ingredients of your pharmaceutical goods.

In addition to the exposure of event data its combination can lead to exposure of business secrets. Recording the complete query history and its analysis builds the basis for adaptation of access rights to prevent exposure of sensitive business secrets. With respect to Hyp. 1, the security extensions are analyzed regarding their response time characteristics in Sect. 5.7.2.

Matthieu-P. Schapranow, *Real-time Security Extensions for EPCglobal Networks,*
In-Memory Data Management Research, DOI: 10.1007/978-3-642-36343-6_5,
© Springer-Verlag Berlin Heidelberg 2014

The given examples for the business-level security extensions are presented in context of RFID-aided supply chains. However, they are designed for EPCglobal networks, i.e. also other techniques for product identification, such as barcode scanner, can build their technology foundation.

5.1 Architecture

I followed a SoD approach during the design process of the architecture. Thus, I developed dedicated components per task that form the architecture of the business-level security extensions as follows:

- **Inquirer:** The querying party asking for details about a certain good,
- **Access Control Client (ACC):** A piece of software installed at the querying party, which enables transparent security extensions for existing EPCIS repositories,
- **EPCIS Repository:** It contains captured event data and processes incoming queries for certain EPCs,
- **Access Control Server (ACS):** It contains access control rules and applies them for a certain query and inquirer,
- **Trust Relationship Server (TRS):** optional component that combines information about specific business partners, and
- **Certificate Authority (CA):** It performs validation of client certificates in context of the PKI.

Figure 5.1 depicts the interaction of the aforementioned architecture components via the Internet. ACC and ACS are responsible for secured data exchange and filtering; TRS provides additional information for decision taking. Figure 5.2 depicts the involved entities of the ACS and their relationships. It shows that the basic access control mechanisms as discussed in Sect. 2.1 are combined in HBAC. RBAC is implemented through user entities that are grouped to role entities

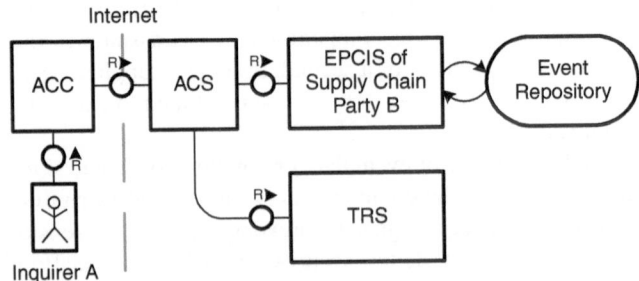

Fig. 5.1 Interaction of HBAC actors to combine RBAC and RuBAC for decision taking (*ACC* Access Control Client, *ACS* Access Control Server, *TRS* Trust Relationship Server)

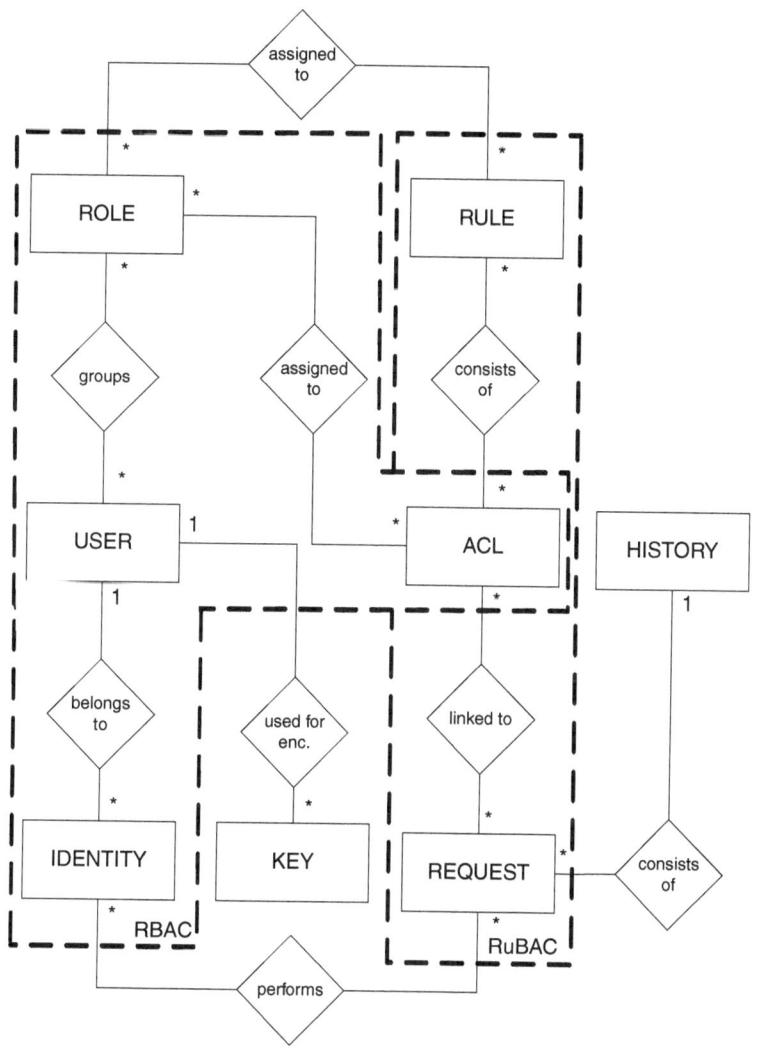

Fig. 5.2 Entity relationship diagram of HBAC. It combines RBAC and RuBAC as basic access control approaches

and `acl` entities, which are assigned to roles instead of users extracted from the history. RuBAC builds on `rule` entities that contain predicates based on `acls`, which are assigned to `role` entities. In the following, I define the functionality of the aforementioned components in further detail.

5.1.1 Inquirer

The inquirer can either be a natural person, e.g. a customer or a business partner, which bought a product. This entity is interested in gathering information about a certain product identified by its EPC or about a reading location identified by its Serialized Global Location Number (SGLN) to validate the product's authenticity. The inquirer is typically neither part of the queried company nor known beforehand. Inquirers communicate with the EPCIS via public interfaces. For example, Simple Object Access Protocol (SOAP) is used to query details of products via the web service of the EPCIS.

5.1.2 EPCIS Repository

The EPCIS repository stores event data captured by reader devices within a certain company or department. It implements standardized interfaces for querying event data defined by EPCglobal [1]. I consider it as a standard software component and its implementation is not considered in further detail.

5.1.3 Access Control Client

The Access Control Client (ACC) is responsible for enforcing access rights and filtering of event data at the inquirer's site. The ACC relays the inquirer's queries via a SSL tunnel to the corresponding ACS of the event owner as depicted in Fig. 5.1. The encrypted result set is received by the ACC from the ACS. Afterwards, rights for accessing data of the result set are requested from the ACS. The ACC performs decryption and filtering of the result set in accordance with the retrieved access rights. As a result, the ACC is responsible to create a client-specific view on the data before returning the filtered event set to the inquirer. With respect to the XACML model, the ACC acts as a PEP [2].

5.1.4 Access Control Server

The Access Control Server (ACS) is the pendant of the ACC and a dedicated instance for rights management on server site. It decouples access control from data contained in the EPCIS repository as depicted in Fig. 5.1. As a result of this design decision, it is possible to change access rights at any time without affecting involved event data. Additionally, the ACS keeps the EPCIS software unmodified since it extends its functionality.

In terms of the XACML model, the ACS acts as PDP [2]. The ACS is the extension point to include external information that influences the decision taking process. For example, the ACS interacts with optional information sources, such as the TRS, when no sufficient decision information for the given inquirer is locally available. In other words, information provided by other PIPs is combined for decision taking by the ACS.

Application Example: Consider an unknown business partner that queries event data from an EPCIS repository for a certain SGLN. With respect to the functional requirement F5 defined in Sect. 3.1.3 the event owner is interested to exchange a minimum of details, i.e. about products sold to the unknown business partner. Instead of providing all event data, the event owner filters and returns only EPC and timestamp of goods that were shipped to the inquirer. This way, the event owner hides the majority of details from the querying business partner. The event owner decides to share additional details about intermediate business steps associated with products shipped to this party after some time. Thus, the inquirer's access rights are updated while the event data remains unchanged.

Implementation: Table 5.1 summarizes entities of the ACS database. The database schema was designed to be applicable for both traditional SQL databases, such as MySQL, and in-memory databases, such as SAP's in-memory database. The table acls holds entities that were extracted from incoming queries, which are relevant for access control. All incoming requests of inquiring parties are appended to the history table. Any querying party, e.g. a company, is mapped to a concrete user. A user is an abstraction for a certain inquirer of the EPCIS identified by an X.509 certificate subject. Users can have multiple identities, e.g. departments of the same company with individual ACCs that perform individual queries. An identity is a certain ACC identified by its certificate fingerprint. For encryption of event data, user-specific keys are stored. The table roles builds the basis for the implementation of RBAC as described in Sect. 2.1. Rules are used to specify a combination of business secrets that need to be protected. A rule consists of a list of

Table 5.1 Entities of the ACS and a brief description of their function

Table	Description
acls	Complete history of assets and requested actions
acls_roles	Mapping of assets, actions and roles
history	Complete history of all ACS requests
identities	All individual identities
identities_requests	Mapping of identities and requests
identities_users	Mapping of identities and users
keys	Complete history of all encryption keys
keys_users	Mapping of keys and users
roles	List of roles
roles_rules	Mapping of roles and rules
roles_users	Mapping of roles and users
rules	List of rules
users	Complete history of users

permissions and/or prohibitions. One or multiple rules are assigned to user groups. Users are assigned to one or multiple groups. Access rules are used for HBAC. Remaining database tables exist for schema normalization.

5.1.5 Configuration Tool

The security administrator is responsible for configuration of the security extensions. This requires configuration of the policy base, which defines the system behavior. Through a web interface the security administrator can access the policy base from a variety of devices, e.g. desktop PC or smartphone. This configuration tool is referred to as PAP in terms of the XACML model [2]. The configuration tool is used to create new rules, check current system functionality, and to analyze the history of queries to detect possible data leakages, as it was defined as part of the functional requirements in Sect. 3.1.3. With its help, the security administrator is able to specify rules to protect business information. Rules consist of regular expressions that define information that need to be protected. If multiple rules match, the HBAC adapts the current access decision individually by analyzing the query history of the specific inquirer. The configuration tool addresses the non-functional requirement N3 defined in Sect. 3.1.3 to minimize configuration time of the HBAC.

5.1.6 Trust Relationship Server

In context of my work, I refer to *trust* as the absence of complete certainty. The Trust Relationship Server (TRS) is implemented to provide a client-specific scoring algorithm. With the help of rules, the reputation of an unknown inquirer is evaluated and a specific score is derived. The interaction with remote TRSs is depicted in Fig. 5.3. With reference to the XACML model, the TRS acts as a PIP [2].

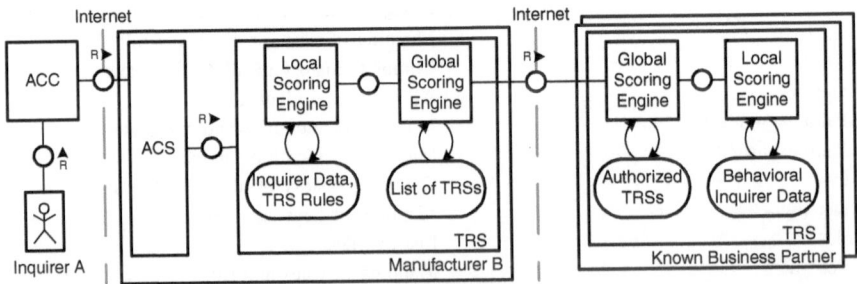

Fig. 5.3 TRS connects to remote TRSs of predefined business partners to acquire additional information about new inquirers (*ACC* Access Control Client, *ACS* Access Control Server, *TRS* Trust Relationship Server)

Application Example: Let us assume an unknown inquirer A that requests details for one of your products. With respect to functional requirement F5 it is a risk to provide arbitrary information to A. Thus, the ACS involves the TRS component in the decision taking process. The TRS connects to a predefined list of TRSs of known business partners and queries for any details about A. If any of the known business partners has performed business actions with A behavioral data is stored. The remote TRS evaluates the behavioral data of A and returns a specific scoring. If any suspicious business behavior is recorded for A, the specific score is low, whereas positive business experiences result in a positive score. The TRS of manufacturer B applies company-specific trust rules to all received scores. As a result, a single score for the unknown inquirer is returned to the ACS, which influences the initial negotiation of access rights or decision taking for known inquirers.

I refer to this collaborative approach that acquires a specific trust scores for unknown supply chain parties as *federated trust*. It builds a basis for addressing the function requirement F5 as defined in Sect. 3.1.3. Thus, the ACS is able to filter event data for new and unknown inquirers accordingly to business experiences recorded by other business partners. Similar approaches exist for evaluating the payment morale of customer, e.g. SCHUFA score [3].

Implementation: Since the TRS operates as part of a globally interconnected network, suspicious clients or malicious behavior recognized by any supply chain party are logged. Depending on the detected activities, a client-specific score is calculated. The TRS consists of a local and a global scoring engine. The local engine is company-specific and contains details about suspicious behavior of clients that interact with the local company only. The global engine contacts a list of TRSs of predefined business partners, which process the query locally.

5.1.7 Certificate Authority

The Certificate Authority (CA) is required for establishing a PKI. The CA issues certificates for trusted clients and maintains Certificate Revocation Lists (CRLs), e.g. to revoke certificates when keys have been compromised.

Application Example: Clients holding a valid certificate can use the CA to verify their identity or to protect queries against manipulation by using digital signatures. The ACS verifies the identity of certain clients by checking the validity of the inquirer's certificate with the help of the CA. With respect to the functional requirement F4 defined in Sect. 3.1.3 the certificate is used for identification of the inquirer.

5.2 Extended Process Steps

In the following, required process steps of the security extensions are outlined. With its help, the requirements of real-world scenarios are analyzed and subsequent benchmarks are performed. Recording each querying party and its queries q_u is performed to build a history of requests and to adapt access rights individually as described in Sect. 5.4.

New Inquirer
In the context of this dissertation, I refer to *inquirers* as all kinds of business partners, e.g. wholesalers, retailers, any kind of company. An inquirer u for a given EPCIS *epcis_i* is referred to as new unless the ACS does contain any record identifying u. The first time a new inquirer is performing a query, a user u is created within the ACS, which results in a single insert operation to database table `users`. Another insert operation is performed to map the newly created user to the default rule in database table `roles_users`. A new inquirer is referred to as *default* as long as it is not assigned to any business role r_u in the ACS of the business partner. In other words, a default user is known by the ACS but does not hold access rights other than specified by the default role.

New Identity
I refer to an *identity* as concrete actor of an inquirer that performs queries, e.g. an ACC installed of certain department. The first time an ACC of an unknown inquirer is performing a query, its corresponding identity i_u is created within the ACS. Creating a new identity results in insert operations to the database tables `identities` and `identities_users` to map the new identity to the corresponding user.

Key Creation
If there is no encryption key enc_u for a certain user, a new offset for the AES 256 CBC cipher is generated using the `rand_bytes` PRN generator of the Python M2Crypto library. The enc_u is stored in the database of the ACS and mapped to the user during protocol step three of the communication protocol depicted in Fig. 5.6. Key creation and mapping requires two insert operations (`keys`, `keys_users`).

Existing Inquirer
An existing user u and its identity i_u needs to be retrieved from the database tables `users`, `identities`, and `identities_users`. One of the following alternatives applies:

- If u exists, but i_u is missing, a new i_u is created or
- If u and i_u exist, the current enc_u is retrieved.

Key Retrieval
Result sets need to be encrypted with the user-specific encryption key enc_u. The key is created during user creation and needs to be renewed periodically to prevent attacks against the key itself. The corresponding enc_u is looked up using

the user performing a single join operation on the database tables `keys` and `keys_users`.

Role-Based Access Control in the ACS
Predefined access rights are assigned to users via roles to implement RBAC. Roles are used as an abstraction for one or multiple users. To obtain the set of access rights, i.e. rights and prohibitions, the user's role is identified via a join operation and the associated access rights need to be joined additionally. As a result, two join operations are required to obtain access rights, i.e. a mapping between users and roles and corresponding access rights. In Fig. 5.8, RBAC is used to derive the basic access rights for a certain user during protocol step 11.

Rule-Based Access Control in the ACS
RuBAC is used to implement access rules. Rules are grouped to rule sets, which are assigned to certain roles. Retrieving access rules is performed using a single join operation to obtain rules and corresponding rights. Prohibitions are derived from analyzing the complete query history of an inquirer. In other words, a complete scan of the query history of a specific inquirer is performed and associated rule sets are evaluated. All rules of a rule set are combined using the logical OR operation. If two or more rules of one rule set match, a specific prohibition for the inquirer is automatically derived. Thus, defined rules need to be mutual exclusive. Resulting access rights prohibit access to data that are specified by rules of the matching rule set, which ensures protection of data specified by the rule set. In Fig. 5.8, RuBAC processes access rules to adapt basic access rights retrieved via RBAC during protocol step 11.

Classification of Process Steps
I refer to the process steps for new inquirer, new identity, and key creation as *atomic*. In contrast, I refer to the process step for an existing inquirer as *composed* since it combines one or more of the atomic process steps. Table 5.2 compares required database operations of atomic process steps and its access patterns. Two categories of process steps can be distinguished. Category A consists of process steps that occur mostly once when a new inquirer contacts the ACS. The corresponding database operations are performed during the migration towards security extensions and rarely during regular operation. Category B consists of process steps, which are repeatedly performed every time an inquirer is querying event data.

Table 5.2 Comparison of atomic process steps and database operations. Process steps of category A mainly occur once, process steps of category B occur regularly

Category	Process step	DB Ops.	Occurrence
A	New inquirer	3 inserts	Once for every new user
A	New identity	2 inserts	Once for every new user
A	Key creation	2 inserts	Once for new users / when key renewal occurred
B	Key retrieval	1 join	For every query
B	Rule-based access control	2 joins	For every query
B	Access rule set	1 join	For every query

5.3 Communication Protocol

In the following, I introduce my extension of the standardized EPCglobal communication protocol to underline specific security features. Figure 5.4 depicts a
traditional client-server communication protocol also defined by EPCglobal [1].
Figure 5.5 depicts the full communication protocol of my security extensions
between inquirer A and the EPCIS repository of the product's manufacturer B. In
contrast to the EPCglobal protocol, my protocol is two-divided in event and
license data communication as depicted in Figs. 5.6 and 5.8 respectively.

Event Data Communication
I refer to *event data communication*, when a client contacts the EPCIS to retrieve a
set of event data for a certain *QueryQ*. This is a query response conversation
between ACC and the EPCIS of the event owner as depicted in Fig. 5.6.

Fig. 5.4 UML sequence
diagram depicting traditional
communication protocol for
client-server applications, e.g.
FOSSTRAK query client and
EPCIS repository

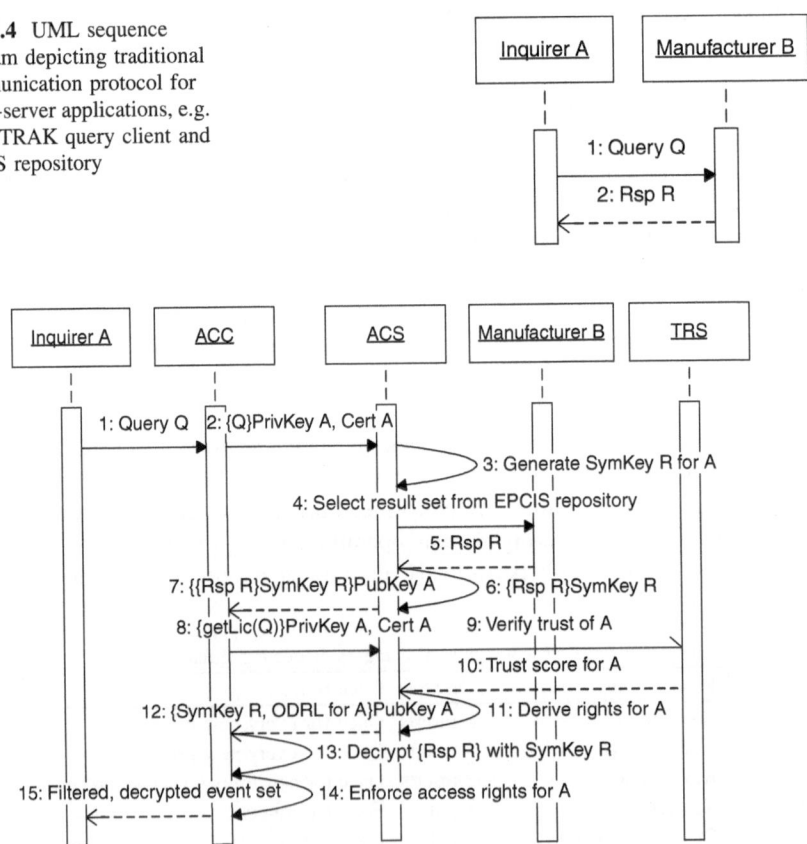

Fig. 5.5 UML sequence diagram depicting the extended communication protocol involving
HBAC components ACC and ACS

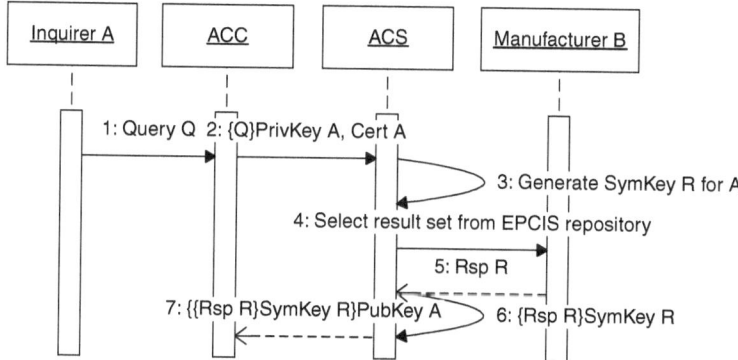

Fig. 5.6 UML sequence diagram depicting the message flow of event data communication in HBAC

Asymmetric Encryption: I restrict EPCIS communication to be performed via SSL links only. Firstly, securing the communication between ACC and ACS prevents eavesdropping of clear text queries and responses. Secondly, the X.509 certificate *CertA* of client *A* is required to establish the encrypted communication channel while sharing public information of the inquirer with the EPCIS. During communication setup the ACC's certificate is verified by contacting the responsible CA as depicted in Fig. 5.7. *CertA* is used by the ACS to identify the ACC and to associate its queries for logging the query history. The ACC performs the same steps to verify the EPCIS' authenticity since the public X.509 certificate of the ACS is also exchanged during SSL handshake. All X.509 certificates are generated with a default key length of 2,048 bits for the RSA public key. This key length was selected with respect to the recommendation of the EPCglobal CP as discussed in Sect. 2.2.

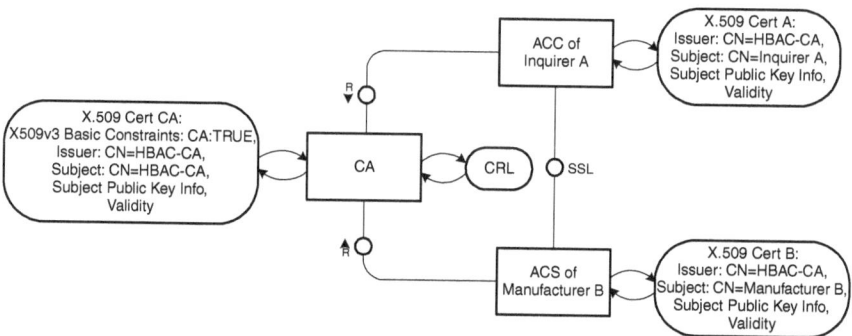

Fig. 5.7 Interaction of ACC, ACS, and CA for authentication (*ACC* Access Control Client, *ACS* Access Control Server, *CA* Certificate Authority, *CRL* Certificate Revocation List). During SSL setup ACC and ACS verify the certificate of its communication partner against the trusted CA. The SSL connection is only established if the mutual authentication was successful

After the successful authentication of the ACC, the EPCIS fetches the relevant set of event data from its repository and creates the response *RspR*. The event set is symmetrically encrypted using an AES 256 CBC *SymKeyR*. The encrypted event set {*RspR*}*SymKeyR* is sent via the SSL connection to the ACC. The interested reader may ask, why event data are encrypted although they are transmitted via a SSL connection. The owner of the event data encrypts it to prevent the client from accessing it unfiltered. To clarify, in response to its query, the client's ACC receives a symmetrically encrypted event set. However, *SymKeyR* is not shared with the ACC itself. If the ACC holds the valid certificate used for SSL session, she/he is able to decrypt the response and ends up with the encrypted data set {*RspR*}*SymKeyR*.

Symmetric Encryption: The design decision to use a symmetric encryption technique was taken with respect to Hyp. 1. Symmetric encryption can be performed faster than asymmetric encryption for a variable length response [4]. The size of the *RspR* depends on the selected event types, EPCs, and supply chain specific factors such as number of involved parties. The decision to incorporate symmetric encryption was taken to have a stable encryption/decryption time for a varying size of *RspR*. The symmetric key is user-specific to prevent expose of mass data in case of a compromised shared key with reference to Hyp. 3. In other words, each ACC receives the event data encrypted by its specific key. For subsequent decryption attempts, the ACC needs to contact the ACS to retrieve the latest symmetric key for decryption. For HBAC, the minimal key length of the symmetric key was set to 64 Bits to prevent brute force attacks against the key.

License Data Communication
License data communication refers to the acquisition of access rights, its enforcement, and the filtering of the result set. Fig. 5.8 depicts the communication

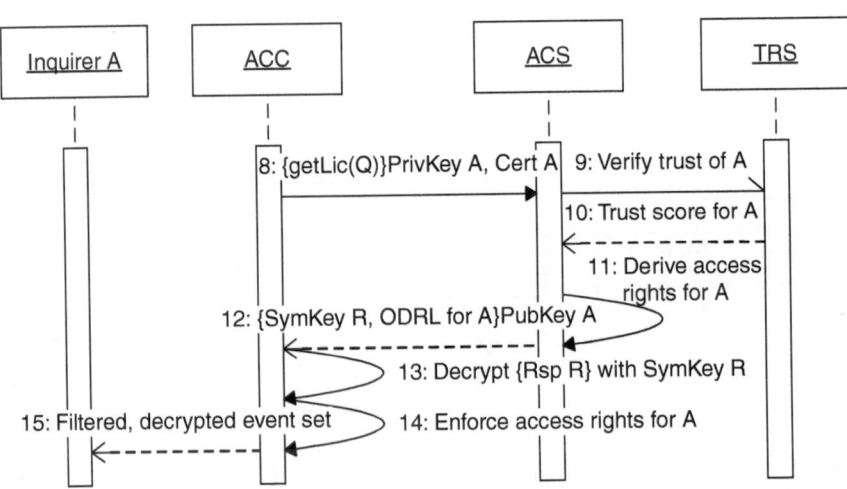

Fig. 5.8 UML sequence diagram depicting message flow of license data communication in HBAC

that is required to receive access rights and to filter results from the encrypted *RspR*.

The ACC specifies an ODRL 2.0 request to retrieve access rights with reference to a certain *QueryQ* [5]. It includes a list of desired permissions that are sent via the SSL connection to the ACS in protocol step eight as depicted in Fig. 5.8. These permissions describe the subset of data the inquirer wants to access and that therefore need to be extracted from {*RspR*}*SymKeyR*. After performing authenticity checks of the client's ACC, the ACS optionally contacts the TRS to evaluate the trust level of querying party A during protocol steps nine and ten. The trust score can be used to adapt access rights for the querying party A specifically. The ACS responds during protocol step 15 with an ODRL response containing details for *SymKeyR*.

Event Filtering: Once the ACC received the details for the symmetric key, it derives *SymKeyR*. With the help of *SymKeyR*, it decrypts *RspR* during protocol step 13. Then, the ACC has full access to *RspR*. Before returning the data to the querying party A, access rights are applied and the result set is filtered during protocol step 14. Finally, only the filtered event set is returned to the querying party.

5.4 Enforcement of Access Rights

I define *access rights* as a set of rules that contain permission or prohibitions for a certain entity to perform certain operations with a set of data. I incorporated the XML-based ODRL 2.0 standard for my security extensions since it is a very lightweight language to express basic access control entities as described in Sect. 2.1. More expressive languages, such as XACML, can be used as an alternative replacement for ODRL. XACML is more expressive than ODRL. However, the transmitted payload is also larger than the payload for a similar ODRL request/ response pair. Due to the larger message size, encryption and decryption of access rights require additional processing time. I incorporated ODRL to minimize communication overhead and to optimize processing time with reference to Hyp. 1.

Listing A.4 in Appendix A.4 depicts an ODRL request for the right to display (line 3) related information about a concrete item identified by SGTIN 1318661593.003.000269655103 (line 4). The first line contains a unique policy identifier, which is stored by the ACS to protocol granted access rights per inquirer. As a result, the ACS is able to reconstruct the complete history of queries for a certain querying party.

The corresponding ODRL response is given in Listing A.5. It consists of two permissions (lines 2–5, 6–9) and one prohibition (lines 10–13). The ACC interprets the asset UID as a regular expression, i.e. a partial matching is sufficient to satisfy either a permission or a prohibition of an ODRL response. For example, the prohibition uid = "T1[0-5]" in line 12 restricts access to events with timestamps from 10h00 to 15h59. Multiple permissions or prohibitions are combined via a logical OR operation, i.e. a single matching rule of a rule set is sufficient for filtering. For filtering, prohibitions are firstly and permissions are secondly applied, i.e. whitelisting is performed to ensure that explicitly assigned permissions are not impeded by HBAC. Enforcement of access rights is two-fold: (a) calculation of a trust score and (b) evaluation of the query history.

Trust Score: The client-specific trust score is the outcome of the mathematical function *trust* that assigns a concrete business partner p a numeric representation from interval $[0, 1]$ with the interpretation [low, high] as given in Eq. 5.1.

$$trust(p) \mapsto [0, 1] \tag{5.1}$$

Based on company-specific experiences with a certain business partner, a specific trust score is maintained by the TRS. If an unknown inquirer makes contact for the first time, the TRSs of predefined business partners are contacted to include their potential experiences with the new inquirer and to derive a global trust score. Thus, a specific trust score for each inquirer can be calculated by combining local and global trust scores using company-specific trust rules.

History Evaluation: The ACS records the history by logging all incoming ODRL requests. Minutes, days, or weeks after the first query, a second query can be used for combination of sensitive data. Thus, it is mandatory to keep a complete history of queries without deletion. During creation of the corresponding ODRL response, the history is evaluated using access rules to detect potential exposure of business secrets. Once a rule is violated, access rights are adapted accordingly to prevent further exposure of data.

5.5 Security Evaluation

In the following, architecture components and actors of the HBAC are evaluated regarding their capability to resist certain threats and attacks as introduced in Sect. 3.1. The evaluation addresses information security aspects individually.

Query/Response between ACC and ACS
Confidentiality: Why is confidentiality of EPCs important although the EPC is considered as the successor of the EAN and the latter was not treated confidentially? In contrast to the traditional EAN that identifies a group of products, an EPC identifies a concrete product instance. In other words, event data are more fine-grained than EAN data. This unique identifier can be used for tracking and tracing of products as well as individuals to expose customer relationships and customer profiles as defined by threat T3 or T4 respectively. In terms of information security, customer profiling by third parties must be prevented to increase the acceptance for EPCglobal networks. I consider customer's privacy worthy of protection.

Integrity: Due to the Internet connection between inquirer and queried EPCIS repository, confidentiality of queries needs to be considered separately. I make use of asynchronously encrypted SSL connections between ACC and ACS. The use of SSL connections guarantees the integrity of data between communication peers. Securing further actors of EPCglobal networks, such as the ONS, is addressed by related work [6].

Authentication: From the EPCIS's perspective, it is important to identify querying parties, e.g. the querying ACC. Firstly, result sets are filtered specifically for each ACC. For example, an unknown querying party receives only information that a certain product was handled or manufactured. In contrast, well-known business partners also receive details about the manufacturing time, the inventory location or involved supply chain parties. Secondly, the EPCIS wants to identify each ACC to keep track of shared data as motivated by Hyp. 2. From the inquirer's perspective, it is also important to know who performed which queries and received corresponding result sets. For example, confidentiality of queries need to guaranteed to prevent exposure of customer relationships as defined in threat T4 in Sect. 3.1.

I incorporate a dedicated PKI for authentication purposes, i.e. each supply chain party holds a unique X.509 certificate as depicted in Fig. 5.7. The X.509 standard defines the format of digital certificates of PKI and its operation [7]. EPCglobal does not recommend to use X.509 certificates for authentication purposes specifically. The CP contains recommendations about how to include locations, devices, and service information only [8]. For authentication purposes, I incorporate a dedicated PKI including a trusted CA. Clients need to authenticate its identity using an X.509 certificate containing personal information. Listing A.1 in Appendix A.3 shows an excerpt of an X.509 certificate in textual format, which contain attributes, such as `Issuer`, `Validity`, or `Subject` as depicted in Fig. 5.7. Before creating a Certificate Signing Request (CRS), an asymmetric RSA key pair is created. The requester of the certificate only knows the private key of the key pair. The public key is part of the certificate and can be used by any third party to exchange encrypted data with the owner of the certificate. In contrast to symmetric encryption, which requires the knowledge of a shared secret by all communication partners, asymmetric encryption does not require the exchange of a shared secret before communication. X.509 certificates are piggy packed during setup of the SSL connection, i.e. the ACC and the ACS need to hold a valid certificate issued by the trusted CA or any delegate to setup a communication channel. The X.509 certificates are verified during connection setup, i.e. the CRL of the responsible CA and certificate attributes are checked, e.g. `Subject`, `Not Before`, and `Not After`. The exchange of data starts only after successful verification of both connection peers, which addresses the functional requirement F3 as defined in Sect. 3.1.3.

Access Rights
The functional requirement F2 as defined in Sect. 3.1.3 addresses access control. Thus, access rights specify, which portion of data to filter before returning to the inquirer [9].

Confidentiality of access rights and authenticity of communication partners are protected in HBAC by design. Access rights are only exchanged via a secured SSL connection. Thus, the integrity of exchanged messages is guaranteed since both communication peers are directly connected via the encrypted channel. The interception of exchanged messages is not possible.

Event Data

I separated data retrieval and enforcement of access rights from each other. The proposed architecture incorporates the functionality of an ACS that implements access control in a transparent way. Access rights are enforced at the latest possible point in time by the ACC on the client site. On the one hand, the late enforcement of access rights introduces potential threats. On the other hand, this separation has major advantages. For example, updated access rights are directly populated to the ACS. The next time the ACC queries the ACS they are enforced without any latency, e.g. marshaling within the network stack. Even when the event set was retrieved before the client's access rights were updated the event set is filtered accordingly to the latest valid access rights.

Event data are exchanged through SSL connections and additionally encrypted using a symmetric key. In other words, even the ACC receives encrypted event data. As a result, the ACC cannot decrypt the message unless the ACS is contacted and returns details to derive the decryption key.

Due to the separation of event data and enforcement of access rights, the entire result set needs to be sent to the ACC. The latter performs data decryption and enforces access rights. However, compromising the ACC must not result in exposure of event data. Therefore, the symmetric key is only sent after the ACS was contacted. Once the key has been sent to the ACC, event data are decrypted and filtered accordingly to the access rights. During this phase of the communication the entire event data resides in an unencrypted format in the main memory of the server running the ACC software.

The interested reader may understand the presence of the completely unencrypted data set as a potential attack vector. The design decision to perform decryption and rights enforcement on the client site is taken due to load considerations with respect to the non-functional requirement N1 as defined in Sect. 3.1.3. Enforcing access rights on the server site requires additional computational power. As a result, manufacturers and wholesalers, which handle most of the goods within the supply chain, would need to invest in a more powerful IT landscape.

The given security extensions were designed to keep server-site computational power at a minimum. As a result, decryption of event data and enforcement of access rights was moved to the ACC. Furthermore, the need for revoking access rights after event data have been exposed requires a very late enforcement of access rights. For example, once a client acquired event data and potentially caches the result set for further processing, the event owner still has full control over exposed event data. Since every decryption of event data requires acquisition of ODRL access rights, the owner of the event data may change access rights even when data were already returned to the ACC. It restricts data leakage, e.g. the exposure of the ACC certificate or attacks against the ACC software. Data leakages might be detected either on the client site by intrusion detection systems or on the server site, e.g. by monitoring the queries per client and hour ratio. The very late enforcement of access rights is the foundation of restricting further access to sensitive business data. The late enforcement of access rights addresses the requirements of my Hyp. 3. For example, the user-specific symmetric key *SymKeyR* is rotated regularly to limit the success of brute-force attacks against the key, ACC, or ACS.

However, the decision to incorporate symmetric instead of asymmetric encryption was taken with respect to encryption and decryption performance. From a performance's point of view, symmetric encryption is preferable since asymmetric encryption requires more time to process long data chunks [4]. However exchange of the changed key is challenging. I tried to minimize the impact of an exposed symmetric key with respect to Hyp. 3. Individual keys per user, which are rotated hourly, reduce the impact of exposed encryption keys. If a single ACC was compromised, the attacker is only able to decrypt data received by the ACC within the last hour of its operation. Once data leakage is recognized, either the operator of the ACS or the client notifies the CA. As a result, the certificate of the affected party is added to the CRL and a new certificate will be issued.

Software Components
The presented security extensions introduce additional software components, which need to be considered as new attacks.

Access Control Client: The ACC is a software component located on the client site. As a result, it cannot be controlled directly by the event owner and can be attacked without the knowledge of the event owner. Furthermore, attackers could create faked ACC software and run them instead of the verified piece of code. Additionally, attackers can try to attack ACCs instead of the event owner's EPCIS to access the content of the main memory during the decryption phase.

All these examples are attacks against the software code, which have in common that the attacker requires access to the IT system the ACC is running on. Thus, a strict control of the networking layer and the physical hardware prevents most of these attack scenarios. These attacks are identical for existing enterprise systems. As a result, these issues are already addressed by existing company-wide IT policies. Furthermore, it is possible to prevent most of these issues by integration in existing business processes. For example, the event owner does not grant access to event data for all existing ACCs. More realistic, an unknown supply chain party needs to negotiate business relationships initially. In context of this initial negotiation of their mutual business relationship, the ACC of the new business partner is added to the list of known ACCs that are allowed to connect to the ACS. This enables a matching of supply chain parties and corresponding uniquely identified ACCs.

Access Control Server: With respect to the non-functional requirement N1 defined in Sect. 3.1.3 the ACS was designed with minimal server-side load in mind. As a result, the availability of event data in the EPCIS is ensured since the impact of attacks on this software component is reduced. The ACS is exposed to supply chain parties comparable to any other kind of Internet services today. As a result, this service suffers from typical Internet attacks, such as DDoS attacks.

I consider Internet attacks as well understood and existing protection mechanisms, such as firewall rules, VPNs, and high availability of service, can be applied for ACS in a comparable way. These security mechanisms are out of scope of this work. Please refer to existing literature for further details [10].

5.6 Applicability to Existing Event Repositories

The architecture presented in Sect. 5.1 is designed for enhancing existing EPCglobal networks. To verify its applicability in real-world scenarios, I applied them to the open source EPCIS repository of the Free and Open Source Software for Track and Trace (FOSSTRAK) project [11].

FOSSTRAK provides an EPCglobal-certified open-source EPCIS repository developed in Java2Enterprise Edition, which is hosted by an Apache Tomcat Web Application Server [12]. In the following, I share the extension points for the FOSSTRAK EPCIS repository with respect to my security extensions.

Integration: Figure 5.9 depicts the integration of my security extension in the FOSSTRAK EPCIS repository. To integrate them in FOSSTRAK, I developed the FOSSTRAK ACC and ACS. I decided to apply a communication proxy design pattern instead of a direct integration of the security extensions in existing FOSSTRAK code to keep the FOSSTRAK implementation unchanged [13]. Thus, there is no need for code recompilation of existing code. The FOSSTRAK

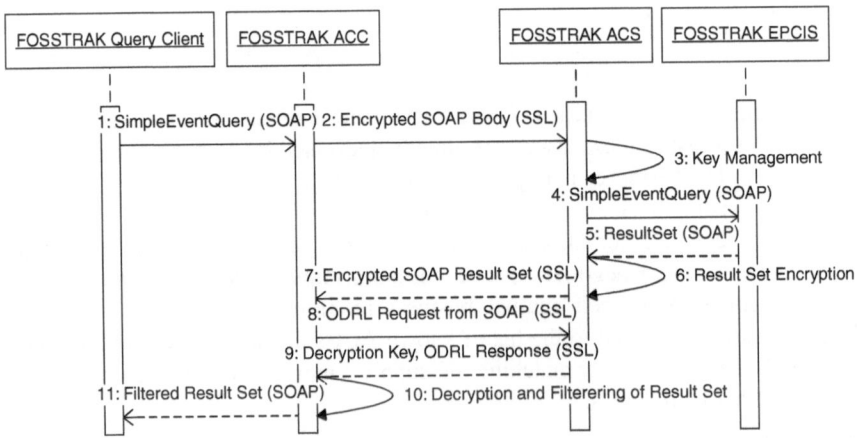

Fig. 5.9 UML sequence diagram depicting message flow for integration of HBAC with existing FOSSTRAK components FOSSTRAK query client and FOSSTRAK EPCIS

implementation offers a query client, which is used to specify queries for the EPCIS repository with the help of a graphical user interface. The URL of the EPCIS repository to query is specified in the client software. Exchanging the URL of the EPCIS by the URL of the FOSSTRAK ACC activates security extensions therefore. This is the only integration effort on client site to activate the transparent security extensions. With respect to the non-functional requirement N4 defined in Sect. 3.1.3, the transparent design reduces required integration efforts on the client site.

Protocol: The FOSSTRAK query client uses SOAP as the communication protocol to exchange data with the EPCIS repository. Incoming client queries are received by the FOSSTRAK ACC and forwarded via a SSL tunnel to the FOS-STRAK ACS in protocol step two as depicted in Fig. 5.9. The incoming SOAP message is forwarded without modifications to the assigned FOSSTRAK EPCIS repository. The ACS extracts control data, such as querying party and queried EPCs, and appends them to the query history. The FOSSTRAK EPCIS repository returns the result set encoded as a SOAP message, which is encrypted during protocol step six and forwarded to the FOSSTRAK ACC. The FOSSTRAK ACC requests proper access rights by creating an ODRL request in protocol step eight. The FOSSTRAK ACC derives the ODRL request by parsing the SOAP message and extracting access control data. The ODRL request is sent via the SSL tunnel to the FOSSTRAK ACS. Its response contains an ODRL response and details of the key for decryption of the retrieved result set.

SOAP to ODRL: The seamless integration of the security extensions within the FOSSTRAK architecture requires deriving access control requests from the existing communication protocol between inquirer and EPCIS repository. Listing A.2 in Appendix A.4 shows a Simple Event Query embedded in a SOAP message. The query consists of three attribute-value pairs enclosed in a `param` section (lines 6–9, 10–15, 16–21), which are combined via the logical AND operation. The result set consists of events that are greater or equal a certain time (`GE_eventTime`) with a certain action (`EQ_action`) and match with a certain EPC code (`MATCH_epc`). Listing A.3 shows an excerpt of the corresponding result set. It consists of events for action `OBSERVE`, i.e. observe events. The Extraction of relevant rights information from the Simple Event Query and its mapping to the corresponding ODRL 2.0 XML dialect is given in Table A.9. It forms the basis for the corresponding XSLT performed by the FOSSTRAK ACC.

5.7 Performance Analysis

On the one hand, increasing security of data is desirable. On the other hand, any kind of security extension has an individual impact on the overall response time behavior of the extended system. With respect to the functional requirements defined in Sect. 3.1.3, I consider response time characteristics as a major factor to investigate for the presented security extensions. In the following, performance characteristics of the presented business-level security extensions are analyzed. A formal analysis of throughput factors is performed in Sect. 5.7.1. Benchmarks addressing the response time behavior of the security extensions are conducted and evaluated in Sect. 5.7.2.

5.7.1 Formal Throughput Characteristics

In the following, I define performance aspects of the business-level security extension for event repositories.

Response Time Requirements
Referring to Hyp. 1 the processing of access rights must not exceed a two second threshold. As a result, the ACS is equipped with a constant monitoring of response time performance. Processing of every query is monitored in terms of response time. After returning the result set to the inquirer, the ACS analyses the timing results. A hysteresis threshold defines the upper threshold for the threshold response time. In the developed system this threshold is set per default to 0.5 s to satisfy the desired overall response time behavior. Every time the measured response time exceeds the desired, a hysteresis counter is incremented. Once a configurable limit of 300 subsequent queries was not processed in the desired response time the ACS explicitly triggers a database optimization and the security administrator is notified. The concrete database optimization operation depends on the incorporated database system. For example, the in-memory database performs a merge operation to build a read-optimized main storage, which is triggered by a dedicated SQL statement [14, Sect. 5.4.2]. Additionally, a splitting of data into several parts or the activation of additional ACS and database instances can be initiated. The implemented response time monitoring forms the basis for various kinds of signaling and optimization tasks. Thus, either automatic or semi-automatic countermeasures can be performed to improve response time. However, database optimizations are not part of this work and are not discussed in further details.

Formal Database Growth and Access Patterns Considerations
Keeping a complete query history for decision taking results in a constantly increasing database size. Clearly, the size of the developed history affects the overall response time of the security extension. I consider the growth of the database as the primary source for an increase in response time. From an engineering perspective, the following operational factors of the security extensions are considered in a formal way and their impact is evaluated.

- q describes the number of queries,
- q_u describes the number of unique queries,
- i describes the number of unique identities,
- u describes the number of unique users,

- k describes the number of encryption keys,
- r describes the number of unique roles in the system, and
- c describes the number of rules.

The following unequations are derived from the concrete requirements of the pharmaceutical industry outlined in Sect. 1.1:

- $q_u < q$, i.e. if a certain good is queried once, subsequent queries for this product can be expected, e.g. the are performed by all supply chain parties that handled the good during goods receipt,
- $u < i$, i.e. identities are used to distinguish individual ACCs of a user u, e.g. departments of a single company,
- $k = u$, i.e. users need encryption keys for secure exchange of data, and
- $r < u$, i.e. users are assigned to roles to abstract from the amount of unknown inquirers. I assume a relatively small number of roles to be in place, e.g. dedicated roles for suppliers, customers, and unknown parties.

A summary is given in Eq. 5.2, which can be used to estimate database size increases.

$$r < u < i, q_u < q \qquad (5.2)$$

Table 5.3 shows the expected growth of database tables and access patterns incorporated by HBAC. It shows that readings are the dominant access pattern. Most database tables are updated once, e.g. for a new user, inquirer, key, etc. However, the majority of data is read, e.g. to evaluate the query history, access rules, etc. These access characteristics fit best for the incorporated in-memory

Table 5.3 Expected growth of database tables incorporated by HBAC. Access patterns are dominated by readings. Insert or update operations occur mostly once

Table	Growth	Access pattern
history	Increases with n	WORM, for logging and archiving only
identities	Increases with i	1 x INSERT per identity, multiple readings
identities_users	i entries	1 x INSERT per identity/user, multiple readings
keys	k entries	1 x INSERT per user or key rotation, multiple readings
keys_users	k entries	1 x INSERT per pair of key and user, multiple readings
roles_users	r entries	1 x INSERT per user, updates possible, multiple readings
users	u entries	1 x INSERT per user, multiple readings
acls	a entries	1 x INSERT, multiple readings
acls_roles	a entries	Multiple ACLs inserted for a single role, updates possible, multiple readings
identities_requests	n entries	1 x INSERT per unique query
roles	r entries	1x INSERT during role creation, multiple readings
roles_rules	$\leq max(c, r)$ entries	1x multiple rules inserted for a single role, updates possible, multiple readings
rules	c entries	1 x INSERT per rule creation, updates possible multiple readings

Table 5.4 Sizing of the European pharmaceutical supply chain taken from [15]

Entity	Quantity
Manufacturers	2.2 k
Wholesalers	50 k
Retailers	140 k
Goods	30 billion / year

technology. It improves database readings compared to traditional database systems [14, Sect. 5.4].

I present concrete growth estimations for the database volume with the help of concrete assumptions for the European pharmaceutical supply chain. The following example shows the growth estimation for one pharmaceutical manufacturer. The supply chain length is $l = 4$, i.e. goods pass one manufacturer, two wholesalers, and one retailer with the sizing assumptions for the European pharmaceutical supply chain as given in Table 5.4.

With the help of the manufacturer's role, I exemplarily outline the complexity in handling sensitive business data in the correct way. Let us assume a fully mashed supply chain, i.e. each of the involved supply chain parties has potential business relationships with each of the remaining parties. Each supply chain party has a maximum of approx. 192k inquirers querying event data for manufactured or handled goods. Furthermore, let us assume that all manufacturers produce equal amounts of the yearly 30 billion goods. It results in about 13.5 million items per manufacturer and year. For anti-counterfeiting, the manufacturer's EPCIS repository is queried by each of the three succeeding supply chain parties at least once, which results in a total of approx. 40.5 million queries per year as defined in Eq. 5.3 or 111 k queries per day when assuming 24/7 production. Each of the incoming queries can be originated from one of the $u = 192k$ unique business partners.

$$q_u = 13.5M, q = (l - 1)q_u = 40.5M \qquad (5.3)$$

For anti-counterfeiting, all involved parties are expected to verify their goods during goods' receipt by querying event data from all preceding supply chain parties to reconstruct the virtual product history. Pharmaceutical manufacturers do not have direct business relationships with all supply chain parties that handle their pharmaceutical goods. However, all of them query the manufacturer's EPCIS repository to retrieve product details. For example, a concrete pharmacy buys their pharmaceutical products from a pharmaceutical wholesaler. Although the pharmacy does not have direct business relations with the manufacturer, it contacts the manufacturer when a new products is received to verify the product's authenticity.

The variety of unknown inquirers results in the need for initial access rights assignment. Its administrative overhead is time-consuming and requires dedicated personnel to maintain access rights. With respect to the non-functional requirement N2 defined in Sect. 3.1.3 the administrative overhead for managing access rights should be minimized. An automatic exchange of event data is the basis for establishing anti-counterfeiting. However, exchanged event data must not expose business secrets. A combination of the aforementioned requirements motivates an automatic decision taking for access control of event data while enabling automatic data exchange.

The presented security extension introduces various ways to reduce the administrative complexity. For example, RBAC is incorporated to abstract from individual inquirers with identical requirements and reduces the need for assignment of individual access rights. Multiple users are assigned to individual roles and access rights are applied to roles instead of individual users. Once a small set of roles is established, new business partners are assigned to roles while corresponding access rights are automatically assigned to them.

Query History
A complete history of incoming queries needs to be stored by the ACS for granting individual access rights. For every incoming query, the complete query history of a certain client is scanned and checked whether access rules match as implementation of RuBAC. Storing the entire query history results in increasing storage requirements. However, keeping only a partial history results in incomplete facts for decision taking.

Referring to Sect. 3.4, the following in-memory building blocks are incorporated in context of my work and enable the processing of the complete query history in real-time.

- **Columnar Store:** The columnar store is the basis for lightweight compression and partitioning. As a result, selected database columns can be assigned to individual CPU cores or blades systems.
- **Insert-only:** I assume queries to arrive in chronological order. As a result, they are appended in a sorted way to the end of the query history. Since the complete history needs to be stored, new data are appended while none of the existing entries are deleted.
- **Lightweight Compression:** I assume queries that mainly differ in the queried EPC, i.e. queries are similar in terms of complexity and content. Because of this similarity, lightweight text compression techniques, such as dictionary encoding, can be applied to reduce storage requirements of the history. Data are automatically compressed by the in-memory database, which reduces the total storage demands.
- **Partitioning:** Due to the steadily increasing length of the history, splitting the complete history in partitions located on different cores or servers results in smaller portions of data to process. Each of the portions of the history can be accessed individually, which is a basis for parallel executions of database scan operations.
- **Multi-core and Parallelization:** Parallel execution of search queries is possible when a complete table scan is required, e.g. a certain predicate needs to be checked against all entries. Performing a parallel search on similar long chunks instead of a single long database table reduces the total traversal time compared to a single traversal.

5.7.2 Benchmarks

In the following, I present the results of the performed benchmarks to evaluate the applicability of the developed security extensions to the pharmaceutical supply chain discussed in Sect. 1.1. Since the developed security extensions are designed for a transparent use, I focus on the impact on the overall response time when querying event data from an EPCIS repository.

Benchmark Setup

All database benchmarks were conducted on a SAP NewDB database installation also referred to as in-memory database. Relevant version information is 1.50.00.353798 s (dev) built on Sep 1, 2011. In addition, benchmarks for MySQL were performed with MySQL 5.1.49 built on Jul 9, 2010. The operating system was openSuSE 11.2 installed from the official DVD ISO image. The underlying hardware systems are Fujitsu PRIMERGY BX924 S2 blades equipped with two Intel Xeon X5670 CPUs running at 2.93 GHz clock speed. Each of the 64-bit CPUs is equipped with 64 kB L1, 256 kB L2, 12 MB L3 cache size, six CPU cores, 12 CPU threads per CPU, and two QPI links forming a total of 24 available CPU threads per blade [16, Sect. 1.1]. Each QPI link represents a double-pumped data bus, which is operated at CPU frequency up to 3.2 GHz in unidirectional mode and has a payload bandwidth of 16 bits [17]. As a result, main memory or cache content can be theoretically accessed in a single direction at a throughput rate of 11.72 GB/s independently from the associated memory controller and CPU for the given benchmark system as defined by Eq. 5.4. Twice the throughput can be achieved due to the unidirectional mode. However, additional protocol overhead needs to be considered specifically. Blades are equipped with 18×8 GB DDR3 RDIMM running at a maximum frequency of 1,333 MHz forming a total of 144 GB main memory capacity per blade. The network connectivity is achieved through 4-port mezzanine Ethernet network interface cards with a max. bandwidth of 1 GB/s. Benchmarks across multiple blades were performed on instances of identically configured blade systems connected via unmanaged 1 GB/s network switches.

$$2.93\,\text{GT/s} \cdot 16\,\text{bit} \cdot 2(\text{double-pumped}) = 93.76\,\text{GB/s} = 11.72\,\text{GB/s} \qquad (5.4)$$

The FOSSTRAK EPCIS repository version 0.5.0 build on Dec 28, 2010 was used for the benchmarks [11]. Its Hibernate implementation, i.e. the object relational mapper, was adapted to make use of a dedicated instance of the in-memory database in the aforementioned version and settings. The simulator described in Sect. 3.2.2 was used to generate realistic event data for a 1,000:1 and a 2,000:1 model of the European pharmaceutical supply. Both models were simulated for a timespan of 30, 180, and 360 days of manufacturing. For individual benchmark results, the identical event set within the FOSSTRAK EPCIS repository was used.

    To capture the response time, a benchmark script written in Python 2.6.2. was executed from a dedicated benchmark server running Linux. The benchmark script loaded a subset of 1,000 predefined EPCs from the FOSSTRAK EPCIS repository

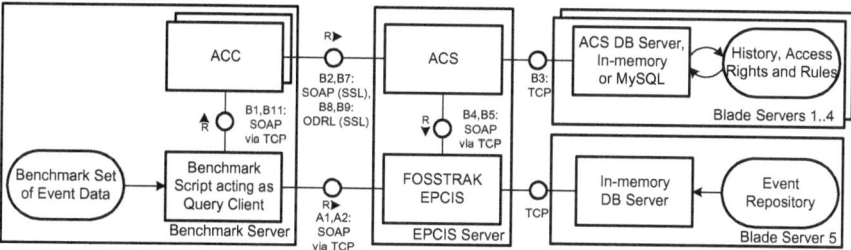

Fig. 5.10 Benchmark Setup for HBAC. Accessing the FOSSTRAK EPCIS requires one network round trip for both: **a** disabled and **b** enabled security extensions. Enabled security extensions require additional network round trips to the ACS database server depending on the incorporated partitioning approach. Protocol steps A1...A2 refer to Fig. 5.4 and B1...B11 refer to Fig. 5.9

into its main memory as benchmark query set. It performed repeatedly the same queries with randomly chosen EPCs out of the benchmark query set. Each query was sent to the FOSSTRAK EPCIS repository either (a) directly or (b) via security extensions as depicted in Fig. 5.10. The response times for disabled and enabled security extensions were measured using python's `time.time()` implementation. The delta of both response time measurements is captured to derive the impact of the security extensions on the overall response time. The precision of the response time measurement depends on the blade's on-board clock's precision. With reference to the Python documentation, the precision of the `time()` function depends on the precision provided by the operating system [18]. An exemplarily output of the `time()` function on the benchmark system is `1328021714.6912911`. As a result, I assume a clock precision of at least $1 \cdot 10^{-6}$ s in the remainder of my work. The captured response time deltas were cleansed by filtering out values outside the interval $]q_{0.9985}, q_{0.0015}[$ with $q_{0.9985}$ defining the 99.85 % quartile, i.e. 99.85 % of all response times are greater than this value. As a result, the interquartile range contains 99.7 % of the recorded values.

Benchmark Configurations
To proof the required real-time response time to satisfy Hyp. 1, I varied the following benchmarks parameters:

- **History Length:** I postulate that the total length q of the query history impacts the overall response time behavior. Thus, the response time was recorded for an increasing history length.
- **Inquirers:** The number of inquirers was varied to proof the lookup time for a small set of relevant queries out of the total history.
- **Partitioning:** To show scalability and extension points of the security extension, range and round robin partitioning policies were selected to measure impact on overall response time behavior.

Table A.10 in Appendix A.5 compares benchmark setups and shows the response time deltas of enabled and disabled security extensions in details. The column partitioning describes the policy used for partitioning of the history. For example, partitioning by 4 ranges across 4 hosts with 4 inquirers results in a single range for each inquirer on each of the four hosts. In contrast, partitioning using round robin 100 across 4 hosts with 10k inquirers results in 100 equally long partitions distributed across 4 hosts. The incorporated partitioning policy affects the reconstruction of the history for a certain inquirer. I configured the total number of partitions less or equal to the total number of available CPU threads, i.e. one CPU thread processes one history partition, which ensures that the system is never fully loaded.

An identical configuration setup of the security extension was chosen for all benchmarks. It consists of a black list role for unknown clients and a default role for known clients. New clients are randomly assigned to the known client's role with an 80 % ratio. Black list clients do not receive any details for their queries. Four static ACLs are specified for the default role using RBAC. One access rule with ten statically defined rules is processed using RuBAC.

Automatic database optimizations of the in-memory database system were disabled. They were triggered by the security extensions if required, i.e. when the hysteresis threshold was exceeded. All data stored in the database were accessed directly without using index structures. As a result, I consider these benchmark results as upper thresholds for the response time. When applying database-specific optimizations, e.g. indexes on the search attribute, the response time behavior can be additionally improved. For example, applying indexes on attributes iden-tities and requests improves mean response by approx. 10 % and the oscillation of response times is lower as depicted in Fig. A.11. However, index structures consume additional main memory capacity and during its creation and update additional processing time is required. I consider index structures as a database-specific optimizations, which are not considered in context of my work and left open for field-test evaluation of the system.

I recommend setting the hysteresis level of the security extensions to a response time that equals the response time after performing the database optimization the first time. Thus, the database optimization is only performed when the response time of the current data layout exceeds the more constant response time of the optimized schema. The concrete hysteresis level is system-specific and needs to be determined per hardware and landscape setup specifically.

Analysis of Response Times

I applied an approximation function given in Eq. 5.5 to derive formal parameters for the comparison of response times. With respect to functional requirement F1 individual approaches are evaluated regarding their response time t for a given length of the query history l_h. Specific parameters b, d are given in Table A.10. Parameter b defines the aspect ratio on the y-axis, whereas parameter d influences the turning point of the graph when the slope turns to less than one. Corresponding approximation functions are plotted for comparison in Fig. 5.11. The benchmark results show that the performance impact of using either round robin or range partitioning is marginal. Local partitioning performs up to 0.2 s better due to the

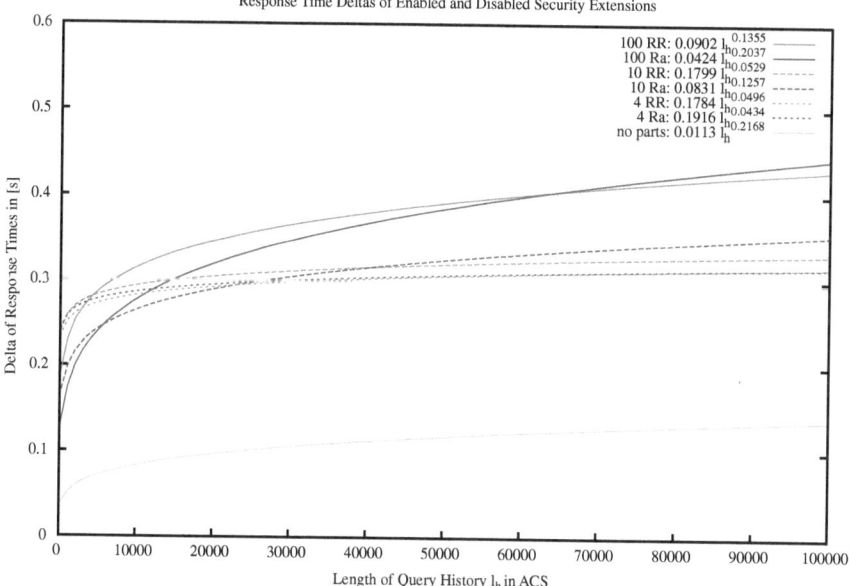

Fig. 5.11 Comparison of HBAC response times for 10 k inquirers using approximation functions. Range partitioning shows better response time behavior in a multi-user system than round robin partitioning due to the lower CPU resources required for analyzing the query history

absence of latency introduced by network communication and data marshaling required for network transmission.

$$rsp(l_h) = b \cdot l_h^{d} \tag{5.5}$$

Parallelization can be used to speed-up the time required to reconstruct the query history for a specific inquirer. The optimal lookup time for a query history that is partitioned across p partitions is defined by Eq. 5.6 when the complexity of its individual lookups equals Eq. 5.7.

$$t = max(t_1, \ldots, t_p), t_i = \frac{t_{table}}{p} \tag{5.6}$$

$$O\left(\sum_{i=1}^{p} O\bigl(process(table_{part_i})\bigr)\right) \leq O(process(table)) \tag{5.7}$$

Round robin partitioning consumes a mean response time of 338 ms in benchmark setup H and 456 ms in benchmark setup J respectively while range partitioning consumes 374 ms in benchmark setup I and 488 ms in benchmark setup J for 10 or 100 partitions respectively as given in Table A.10 in Appendix A.5. This is a comparable low difference of 32–36 ms. Increasing the number of partitions

Fig. 5.12 Summary of mean
HBAC response times for 10k
inquirers based on the
detailed results in Fig. 5.11

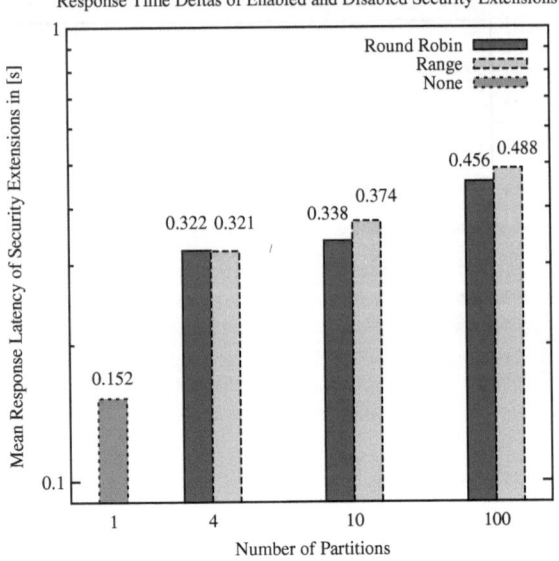

results in smaller data portions per partition that can be scanned faster. Figure 5.12
depicts the comparison of mean responses times. Furthermore, Fig. 5.11 shows in
more detail that 100 partitions perform slower than ten partitions regardless of the
partitioning schema. The development team of the in-memory database confirmed
that this is an issue while pruning the set of data to search. In case of partitioning
the query is split across partitions. After completing the query, the separate result
sets are merged to form the total response. Even if one result set is empty the
merge operation is performed in used database version. Thus, an increased number
of partitions result in processing overhead due to the increased number of result set
to merge. The expected behavior is that the response time improves when
increasing the number of partitions unless the number of partitions exceeds the
number of available physical CPU threads. Due to the smaller data portion to
search per partition, the time to process the complete query is also reduced.

The measured increase in mean response time between 10 and 100 partitions for
the round robin policy is about 118 ms whereas for range partitioning it is only
114 ms. Round robin and range partitioning for four parts show very similar mean
response times of 361 ms in benchmark setup D and 363 ms in benchmark setup
C. In the benchmark setup D, round robin is configured to work comparable to
range partitioning since only a single partition per hosts is available, which prevents parallelization within a single host. For comparison, the mean response time
without partitioning in benchmark setups A and B are approx. 170 ms faster than
any partitioning schema. This improvement of response time is caused mainly by
the absence of any network latency. By implication, the scalability of HBAC
across multiple hosts results only in approx. 170 ms of latency.

Round Robin Partitioning: The benchmarks show that round robin partitioning performs slightly faster than range portioning for all lengths of the query history. On the one hand, incorporating round robin policy guarantees maximum usage of CPU resources. On the other hand, scanning all partitions requires an individual thread per partition to perform the scan. If all queries of a certain client c are equally distributed across p round robin partitions. Its processing time is dominated by the full table scan of the history of all queries within t_{table}. For a single query, each of the p partitions is scanned by a dedicated thread. The optimal processing time t for a single query and p partitions is given in Eq. 5.6. However, for a multi-user system, which processes multiple queries simultaneously, round robin partitioning reduces the overall throughput. Due to the high CPU load—a single CPU thread per partition—parallel processing of queries for multiple inquirers have to be queued. In this case, I consider the high usage of CPU threads as an adverse effect for multi-user systems.

I assume client queries to appear in a random order. As a result, queries of a certain inquirer are not stored equally distributed across all partitions. For example, let us assume only two of ten partitions contain queries of a certain inquirer. A round robin partitioning requires the processing of all ten partitions for reconstruction of the complete history, i.e. a processing overhead of 80 %. In other words, round robin partitioning results in additional processing overhead when incoming queries are not equally distributed. Thus, the power consumption of round robin partitioning is high due to the need for scanning all partitions even when no relevant data is contained.

Range Partitioning: Range partitioning shows very similar response time behavior like round robin partitioning for all benchmark setup. When inserting data to a rage partitioned database table, individual partitions suffer from uneven length with respect to the distribution of inserted values and the amount of queries per inquirer. Similarly to round robin, a single CPU thread processes individual ranges of the partition. If a certain inquirer performs a query, range partitioning benefits from the knowledge, which partition holds the required data.

I assume equally distributed queries with increasing history length. As a result, the individual length of range partitions is also balanced. In contrast to round robin partitioning, only a single CPU thread processes the query since only one partition is required to scan for identification of all queries of a certain inquirer. However, this does not improve the response time. In other words, range partitioning performs better than round robin partitioning for multi-user systems due to a reduced need in CPU resources. Furthermore, range partitioning benefits from a better power efficiency of the algorithm since only relevant partitions are scanned to process a query.

MySQL: In contrast to the incorporated in-memory database, MySQL was used to measure the impact of a traditional database system on the response time of the security extensions. The incorporated database for MySQL is identical to the one used for the in-memory database. Furthermore, it does also not contain any schema optimization, e.g. indexes. It shows that the mean response time of approx. 19 s is about 34-times slower than any of the benchmark results of the in-memory database. Due to the bad response time behavior, benchmarks for MySQL were only performed for the interval $[1, 40,000]$ of history length. The response time for a very small query history is fast, but it increases exponentially due to the required join and union operations. The benchmarks for MySQL were performed without partitioning due to the missing support of the database system. A possible alternative is implementing partitioning policies within the application scope of the security extensions. However, a partitioning management in the application is not part of this work and is left open for further investigations.

Figure A.12 in Appendix A.5 depicts a two-divided graph. For the first interval $[0, 11,500]$, the approximation shows a positive d, i.e. exponential growth. In this interval, new users for the individual 10,000 inquirers are created in the ACS. For the second interval $[11,500, 40,000]$, the approximation function is comparable to its in-memory database pendants with $d < 1$.

Comparison: The length of individual partitions is equally long when using round robin partitioning policy while range partitioning ensures history entries of the same inquirer to be stored within the identical partition. Round robin partitioning requires a scan of all partitions of the history for a certain inquirer since they can be distributed across all partitions. Range partitioning requires only a scan of a single partition since all portions of the history of a single inquirer are stored within the same partition. From a parallelization's point of view, a single CPU thread scans a single partition while multiple CPU threads can scan multiple partitions in parallel. Thus, round robin partitioning results in using a maximum of available computational resources. In contrast, range partitioning consumes less computational resources because only relevant partitions are scanned. Due to the postulated high amount of parallel queries in real-world scenarios as discussed in Sect. 5.7.1, security extensions need to process multiple inquirers in parallel. As a result, range partitioning is preferable in a multi-user system to keep overall load low. The response time behavior of range partitioning is comparable to round robin and therefore an adequate alternative for real-world scenarios. In contrast to traditional databases, the database processing time of an in-memory database is no limiting factor for HBAC. Moreover, partitioning and parallelization are essential scalability factors to analyze the steadily increasing query history and to guarantee a stable response time threshold.

$$bl_h{}^d \leq t_{max} \Leftrightarrow l_h \leq \left(\frac{t_{max}}{b}\right)^{1/d}, \ b, \ d > 0 \qquad (5.8)$$

I used the function given in Eq. 5.5 with the derived parameters from Table A.10 as approximation for the response time. Table 5.5 compares benchmark setups with respect to the maximum history length l_h derived from Eq. 5.8 to meet the response time requirements $t_{max} = 2\,s$ as stated in Hyp. 1. Comparing 100 and ten partitions of individual policies shows that ten partitions process more than eleven orders of magnitude more entries within t_{max}. For 100 partitions the high amount of operating system tasks to manage parallelization and to transfer relevant data via network has

Table 5.5 Comparison of partitioning policies to meet $t_{max} = 2\,s$, no automatic database optimizations (l_h = Max. history length for $l_h \leq t_{max}$)

Setup	Policy	P	H	Inq.	$l_h \vert t \leq t_{max}$
A	None	1	1	4	9.6485e+06
B	None	1	1	10 k	2.3376e+10
C	Ra	4	4	4	5.2128e+06
D	RR	4	4	4	4.3294e+06
E	Ra	4	4	10 k	2.9569e+23
F	RR	4	4	10 k	1.4521e+21
G	Ra	10	4	10 k	9.7699e+10
H	RR	10	4	10 k	5.9311e+19
I	Ra	100	4	10 k	1.6456e+08
J	RR	100	4	10 k	8.5561e+09
K	Ra + idx	100	4	10 k	3.9235e+10
L	MySQL	1	1	10 k	1.8909e+01

a considerable impact on the processing speed. Range partitioning for four partitions has the best processing throughput with a theoretical history length of more than $2 * 10^{23}$ entries for $t \leq t_{max}$. Round robin performs for increasing number of partitions better than the corresponding range partitioning. This is due to the full CPU used by round robin to scan all partitions and the need to merge the results. If the number of partitions exceeds the number of total cores, the high impact of the greedy round robin algorithm will result in a degradation of performance.

With respect to Eq. 5.3, a maximum of $q = 40.5M$ queries per supply chain party needs to be considered. The approximation functions of all benchmarks indicate at least 10^6 queries to be processed within t_{max}. Furthermore, they show that a longer history per inquirer results in longer processing time. The approximation functions for $10k$ clients are representatives of real-world supply chains with $192k$ participants in a ratio of approx. 1:20. Their maximum history length when keeping the response time less than t_{max} is at least two orders of magnitude higher than for four clients.

For benchmarking, the automatic database optimization of the in-memory database was explicitly disabled to eliminate its impact on the results. For example, data compression was not applied to event data. The reduction of data volume when working on compressed data has a beneficial impact on the response time and storage requirements. As a result, I consider the given benchmark results as an upper threshold for the expected response time. In a real-world scenario, I expect database optimizations to be performed on regular basis to constantly optimize access times.

A benchmark considering a high number of distributed clients remains open for real-world field tests. Due to hardware limitations, I was not able to address it in the course of my work.

Columnar Store: Traditional database systems store tuples in rows, i.e. all attributes for a certain row are stored side by side followed by the next row. In contrast, a columnar store holds data of a certain attribute side by side. On the one hand, querying a complete row from a columnar store requires reconstruction of a virtual row, i.e. retrieving individual attributes of the row and link them together as a row. On the other hand, querying only a subset of attributes benefits from a columnar layout since only data involved in the result set need to be accessed. With respect to Fig. 5.2, the following entities are stored in columnar format: `acls`, `history`, `identities`, `identities_requests`, `keys`, `roles`, `rules`, `users`.

Write-Once Read-Many: The insert-only or append-only database table is the implementation of the WORM storage concepts. The latter was developed for archiving purposes. French values WORM devices as high capacity storages, e.g. CD-R, with lower access speed than magnetic disks, but "less prone to data loss than magnetic disks" [19, Sect. 7.18.]. Data stored in this storage is neither updated nor modified. As a result, this kind of database tables fits for bookkeeping purposes since recorded bookings are not allowed to be updated [20]. In context of bookkeeping, data needs to be modified by recording a correction booking. In an insert-only database table, storing a new entry invalidates the existing one but the former value remains stored, i.e. the newest entry for a certain attribute indicates its latest value [21, Sect. 7.1].

For HBAC there is no need to update access logs once they were recorded. Either an inquirer has sent a certain query or not. Once a new query was processed, the history for the inquirer contains the corresponding record. Even if the inquirer did not receive the result, the query was processed and the inquirer might have detailed knowledge about the response. From a security's perspective, this is a properly processed and returned result set for the given query, which has to be recorded in the inquirer's history.

I decided to use a WORM storage to guarantee (a) a persistent history that (b) cannot be modified and (c) modification attempts that are recorded by design, i.e. modifications can be reconstructed if needed.

Compression: The incorporated in-memory database incorporates compression in a transparent way. It is applied to the raw data when the database optimization is triggered. Table 5.6 gives a snapshot of database tables used by the security

Table 5.6 Storage requirements of column database tables ordered by compression factor desc. Database table history compresses best

Table	Records	U [KB]	C [KB]	CF $\frac{U}{C}$
history	520,000	44,536	7,401	6.0176
acls	1,004	189	41	4.6098
identities	10,000	1,757	399	4.4035
identities_requests	520,000	29,894	6,915	4.3231
users	10,000	2,164	557	3.8851
keys	10,000	2,277	825	2.7600
roles	2	12	14	0.8571

U Uncompressed table size, *C* Compressed table size, *CF* Compression factor

extensions with respect to compression. The storage requirements were measured as follows: the automatic database optimization was disabled, the database schema was cleared, database tables were created, and data were inserted. After completing the benchmark, the storage requirements of the uncompressed data (U) were recorded. The compressed data requirements (C) were recorded after triggering an explicit database optimization by the SQL statement UPDATE <TABLE> MERGE DELTA INDEX for the given tables. The compression factor (CF) describes the fraction of storage demands U divided by C. For example, a CF of six describes that the uncompressed data set requires six-times the storage of the compressed data.

Most database tables given in Table 5.6 show a CF of four or more. The history table shows the best CF of 6.02. In other words, an in-memory database is capable to handle six-times the history that can be stored by a traditional database management system with the same storage requirements. I consider this as an important scalability factor. The results show that lightweight compression is one technology aspect that makes my contribution applicable for real-world requirements in context of multi-user systems.

References

1. Global Standards 1, EPCIS Standard 1.0.1 (2007), http://www.gs1.org/gsmp/kc/epcglobal/epcis/epcis_1_0_1-standard-20070921.pdf. Accessed 8 Mar 2012
2. OASIS Open, eXtensible Access Control Markup Language (XACML) V. 2.0. Feb 2005
3. SCHUFA Holding AG, Dept Compass: Empirical Indicators of Private Debt and Over-Indebtedness (2008), http://www.schufa.de/en/media/en/teamenglisch/downloads_11/schufa_debtcompass_2008_englishinternet.pdf. Accessed 8 Mar 2012
4. A.-K. Al Tamimi, Performance analysis of data encryption algorithms (2006), http://www1.cse.wustl.edu/jain/cse567-06/encryption_perf.htm. Accessed 8 Mar 2012
5. ODRL Initiative, ODRL V2.0—XML Encoding (2010), http://odrl.net/2.0/WD-ODRL-XML.html. Accessed 8 Mar 2012
6. J. Sun, H. Zhao, H. Xiao, G. Hu. Lightweight public key infrastructure and service relation model for designing a trustworthy ONS. in *Proceedings of the International Conference on Computer and Information Science*, IEEE Computer Society, 2009, pp. 295–300
7. D. Cooper, S. Santesson, S. Farrell, S. Boeyen, R. Housley, W. Polk. Internet X.509 public key infrastructure certificate and certificate revocation list (CRL) profile (2008), http://tools.ietf.org/html/rfc5280. Accessed 8 Mar 2012
8. Global Standards 1. EPCglobal Certificate Profile Specification Version 2.0 (2010), http://www.gs1.org/gsmp/kc/epcglobal/cert/cert_2_0-standard-20100610.pdf. Accessed 8 Mar 2012
9. M.-P. Schapranow, A. Zeier, H. Plattner. Security extensions for improving data security of event repositories in EPCglobal networks. in *Proceedings of the 9th International Conference on Ubiquitous, Computing*, 2011
10. S.A Tanenbaum, *Computer Networks*, 4th edn. (Prentice Hall, Upper Saddle River, 2003)
11. Fosstrak, Project license (2009), http://www.fosstrak.org/epcis/license.html. Accessed 8 Mar 2012
12. Apache Software Foundation, Apache Tomcat 7.0.16 (2011), http://tomcat.apache.org/tomcat-7.0-doc/index.html. Accessed 8 Mar 2012

13. E. Gamma. *Design Patterns: Elements of Reusable Object-oriented Software.* (Addison-Wesley, Boston, 1995)
14. H. Plattner, A. Zeier. *In-Memory Data Management: An Inflection Point for Enterprise Applications.* (Springer, Heidelberg, 2011)
15. M.-P. Schapranow, J. Müller, A. Zeier, H. Plattner, RFID event data processing: an architecture for storing and searching. in *Proceedings of the 4th International Workshop on RFID Technology—Concepts, Applications, Challenges,* 2010
16. Intel Corporation. Intel Xeon processor 5600 series datasheet (2011), vol. 1, http://www.intel.com/content/dam/www/public/us/en/documents/datasheets/xeon-5600-vol-1-datasheet.pdf. Accessed 8 Mar 2012
17. Intel Corporation. An introduction to the intel quick path interconnect (2009), http://www.intel.com/content/dam/doc/white-paper/quick-path-interconnect-introduction-paper.pdf. Accessed 8 Mar 2012
18. Python Software Foundation, Python V. 2.7.2 Documentation (2012), http://docs.python.org/index.html. Accessed 8 Mar 2012
19. C.S. French, *Computer Science. Letts Higher Education List Series* (Cengage Learning, 1996)
20. L. Pacioli, P. Crivelli, *An Original Translation of the Treatise on Double-Entry Book-Keeping.* (The Institute of Book-Keepers Ltd., New York, 1924)
21. M.-P. Schapranow, Transaction processing 2.0: the epochal change in designing transaction processing systems. Master's thesis, Hasso Plattner Institute, 2008

Chapter 6
Qualitative and Quantitative Discussion

In the preceding chapters, I have presented my contributions for device-level and business-level security extensions for EPCglobal networks. The following section provides a qualitative and a quantitative discussion of my research results. From the systems engineering's perspective, it builds the basis for evaluating the applicability of my security extensions in context of EPCglobal networks.

6.1 Qualitative Improvements

I discuss qualitative improvements of my contribution with respect to EPCglobal networks. Following the structure of the work, this section discusses device-level and business-level security improvements separately. Although I focus on RFID technology as a possible basis for EPCglobal networks, improvements are also valid for use with other technologies, such as barcodes. Please refer directly to Sect. 6.1.2 for a discussion of improvements for business-level security.

6.1.1 Improvements for Device-Level Security

Due to the wide industry spread, I focus on the use of passive UHF RFID tags that comply with EPCglobal generation two respectively ISO 18000-6c for RFID-aided supply chains. From my perspective, this category of tags as described in Sect. 2.2 is promising for use in various industries due to their comparable low manufacturing costs. On the one hand, passive tags come with comparable low manufacturing costs in contrast to semi-active or active tags. On the other hand, these tags come without any integrated security features. As a result, data protection is left open to the user of the tags.

The presented contributions for extending device-level security overcome technical device-level limitations of the tags by introducing mutual authentication

Matthieu-P. Schapranow, *Real-time Security Extensions for EPCglobal Networks*,
In-Memory Data Management Research, DOI: 10.1007/978-3-642-36343-6_6,
© Springer-Verlag Berlin Heidelberg 2014

models in Chap. 4. In contrast to traditional PKIs and asymmetric encryption, mutual authentication protocols require less computational capabilities on the tag. Since both components reader and tags do not know each other within an open supply chain as described in Sect. 3, the presented mutual authentication protocols focus on authenticating the reader against the tag and vice versa. On the one hand, this involves additional computational requirements on the tag. On the other hand, the computational requirements are less than for modern encryption mechanisms [1]. Depending on the expected supply chain length, the static authentication model described in Sect. 4.1 protects RFID tags from being misused by automatically deactivating them once all valid passwords were used. My developed mutual authentication protocols detect improper communication partners and deny access. Updating the current password during authentication and keeping only the active one on the tag reduces on-tag storage requirements.

From the company's perspective, authentication reduces third party attacks by declining access for unauthenticated tags. This prevents anonymous device-level attacks by third parties, e.g. against tags and readers as described by attacks A2, A1, or A4. Furthermore, passive tags can prevent exposure of data to unknown and unauthorized reader devices. Thus, data exchange between unauthorized tags and readers is prevented by design. As a result, the principle of data minimalism is applied to reduce data exchange with unauthorized parties to specifically address cloning and spoofing attacks. The use of OTPs for the dynamic mutual authentication protocol prevents additional replay and man-in-the-middle attacks by design.

6.1.2 Improvements for Business-Level Security

The presented security extensions were designed to improve business-level security. Any kind of anti-counterfeiting implemented in context of EPCglobal networks results in the need for automatic exchange of event data. Therefore, my security extensions focus on EPCIS repositories, which provide standardized interfaces for exchanging event data automatically. However, the automatic exchange of event data results in new threats and attack scenarios as described in Sect. 3.1. As a result, event data need to be considered as sensitive business data from a data protection's point of view. On the one hand, preventing exposure of event data eliminates the risk of misuse. On the other hand, the automatic exchange of event data is required to enable anti-counterfeiting in real-time, which is a competitive advantage for business partners and customers. My security extensions for business-level security address the following aspects:

- **Complete Query History**: A history of queries is recorded to adapt access rights and to prevent exposure of sensitive business secrets defined by access rules. In case of data leakage, the query history can be used to reconstruct the virtual history of the product.

- **Continuous Spectrum of Control**: In contrast to traditional bivalent access control mechanisms the implementation of HBAC enables the use of a continuous spectrum of control. For example, certain elements of event data can be filtered while still providing a valid result set as required by the EPCglobal definition for EPCIS repositories [2].
- **Very Late Enforcement of Access Rights**: The decision to filter data on client-side at the latest point in time supports very fast adaption of access rights, e.g. after a data leakage was detected.

Clearly, the use of transparent security extensions does not prevent all kinds of attack. However, it builds the foundation for automatic control of access based on fine-grained event data. With the help of access rules, it is possible to protect business secrets that must not be exposed. The analysis of the entire query history influences decision taking and makes the outcome specific for each inquirer. By filtering the result set and replacing only confidential data entities, the result set remains integer and can still be used by all applications without any code modifications of existing software. Furthermore, recording the entire query history makes new analytical queries possible. For example, manufacturers and/or wholesalers can use the data to derive supply chain KPIs of their products, such as mean transportation time to client, transportation routes, and details queried for products. This information can be used to improve existing business processes or to detect future business needs. This is the basis for a completely new field of supply chain analysis. The investigation of new KPIs in context of RFID-aided supply chains is left open for further investigation and remains out of scope of this work.

6.2 Quantitative Results

In the following, I discuss quantitative requirements for enablement and operation of RFID-aided supply chains with respect to the motivation given in Sect. 1.1. For a detailed description about my assumptions regarding costs for hardware, software, and individual services, please refer to existing literature [3].

6.2.1 Initial Costs of RFID-Enablement

For RFID-enablement of companies an initial monetary investment is required depending on the roles within the supply chain. For instance, a manufacturer requires both reader and writer devices to initialize RFID tags when new products are produced. In contrast, a retailer only needs to be equipped with reader devices. A detailed classification of expected costs per supply chain role is given in Appendix A.6. Table A.11 compares investments for an on-premise solution with costs of a comparable on-demand solution for setup alternatives of EPCIS repositories. I assume retailers to make use of an on-demand setup to reduce their initial investments to migrate to an RFID-aided supply chain. I split costs accordingly to individual supply chain roles and categorize them using the following criteria [3].

- **Hardware**: Investments associated with infrastructure components for establishing an RFID-aided supply chain, e.g. servers, RFID writing and reading devices, network components, etc.
- **Software**: Investments for software and its required licenses.
- **EPCglobal Fees** Investments to operate as a provider for certain EPC intervals, e.g. EPCglobal license fees [4].
- **Implementation**: Investments, which are required to setup the RFID infrastructure, e.g. costs for consulting, configuration of soft- and/or hardware, implementation tasks, etc.

Role A: Manufacturer: Table A.11 shows, that implementation costs contribute by approx. 80 % to the total costs for supply chain role manufacturer, followed by hard- and software costs with approx. 15 %. Applying a SaaS solution results in reduction of costs for hard- and software components, such as workstations, servers, routers, and special software licenses. Furthermore, implementation efforts for an on-demand solution are reduced since the configuration of existing hardware devices at the manufacturer's site, e.g. RFID reader and writers, is only required on-site. Although these on-site devices are also required in a SaaS solution to scan or to write tags, they exchange data directly with the on-demand solution in the provider's cloud instead of local servers.

A SaaS solution reduces initial investments by approx. 87 % compared to an on-premise solution for the supply chain role manufacturer. Nevertheless, I expect the SaaS approach not to be adopted by manufacturers, because of the related monthly rates. From my perspective, manufacturers benefit from an on-premise solution due to the bulky amounts of annually manufactured products that need to be processed. Moreover, the manufacturer already has a complex IT infrastructure, which is operated regardless of its participation in an RFID-aided supply chain. Its IT landscape consists of various enterprise systems, such as ERP, Inventory Management (IM) or Customer Relationship Management (CRM) systems, operated by trained personnel. Thus, I consider an on-premise scenario without monthly fees as more attractive for manufacturers.

Role B: Wholesaler: The efforts for implementing RFID technology at the wholesaler's site when applying an SaaS solution equals less than 1.5 % of the implementation costs required for an on-premise solution as given in Table A.11. By eliminating the need for huge on-site hardware investments in combination with the lowered administration effort, a SaaS solution helps to save more than 90 % of the initial investments for the supply chain role wholesaler.

I believe, wholesalers are more likely to adopt a SaaS solution more likely, because they are primarily SMEs. The SaaS model is designed for SMEs to reduce investment and operational efforts of the necessary EPCglobal infrastructure. In addition to initial savings, I also expect similarly monthly savings.

Role E: Retailer: Comparable saving potentials exist for retailers. Approx. 93 % of the implementation costs for an on-premise solution can be saved when using an on-demand solution instead as shown in Table A.11. This supply chain role belongs to the SMEs within the pharmaceutical supply chain, which are addressed by a SaaS solution. From my perspective, I expect monthly savings for a SaaS solution to be comparable to the savings for the initial investments.

Cost Evaluation: Building on an on-demand solution has a positive impact on implementation costs. I compared the setup costs per supply chain role within the pharmaceutical supply chain between an on-premise and an on-demand instead of an on-premise solution. Independently from the role within the supply chain, costs savings for the initial investments of 80 % and more can be achieved when applying an on-demand solution. Although the operation of an on-demand solution is connected with monthly operational fees, I believe that the presented reductions of initial investments are the key enabler to increase the adoption of RFID technology while enabling SMEs to participate in RFID-aided supply chains without financial barriers.

6.2.2 Operative Costs of Anti-Counterfeiting

The service provider for anti-counterfeiting depicted as role D in Fig. 1.1 needs to be queried for verification of pharmaceutical items. Each participant of the supply chain can query the service provider in order to verify the authenticity of a concrete product, which is uniquely identified by its EPC. I introduce the metric *"Amount of required network traffic to verify a certain good"* [5]. I assume a concrete pharmaceutical supply chain configuration of length $l = 4$ as follows $1\times$ role A, $2\times$ role B, $1\times$ role E, i.e. a pharmaceutical manufacturer, two wholesalers, and a pharmacy as retailer as shown in Fig. 1.1. For the European pharmaceutical supply chain, I refer to $p = 15$ billion manufactured pharmaceuticals on prescription per year as described in Chap. 5. I assume on-prescription medicines to be initially validated by the service provider. I omit the involvement of boxing, unboxing operations and logistics provider for clarity reasons.

Assuming a retailer who wants to validate a certain product, needs to query the service provider, which identifies all supply chain partners that handled the product. The following communication steps are required:

- Provide the EPC of the good to the service provider, i.e. 12 byte,
- Query EPCIS repositories of all supply chain participants involved in handling the concrete item, which consists of 12 byte per EPCIS repository,
- Receive the response of EPCIS repositories containing the recorded event data for the queried EPC, which I assume to consists of the following four events with an average size of 182 byte [5],

- – 1× event indicating the product's receipt (RECEIVE),
- – 2× events indicating products movements at the party (OBSERVE),
- – 1× event indicating the product's shipment (SHIPPED),

- Receive the response of the service provider containing EPC (12 byte) and authentication information (4 byte).

Equation 6.1 defines the event set for the manufacturer role A, Eq. 6.2 defines the event set stored at EPCIS repositories of roles $r = \{B_1, B_2\}$, which are returned to the service provider, Eq. 6.3 shows the event set of the retailer, which only contains the *receive* event since the product is validated during its receipt.

   In addition to the aforementioned amount of payload, protocol-specific headers need to be considered. I propose UDP as communication protocol since it neither involves latencies introduced by connection setup and teardown times nor a huge protocol overhead such as TCP. It results in an additional overhead for the protocol header of 8 byte for UDP and 20 byte for IPv4 needs to be added to any network query [6]. For clarity reasons, I do not consider any additional overhead, e.g. for a specific application-level protocol or additional authentication details, such as SOAP.

$$E^A = \left\{ e^{A_{received}}, e^{A_{observed_1}}, e^{A_{observed_2}}, e^{A_{shipped}} \right\} \tag{6.1}$$

$$E^r = \left\{ e^{r_{received}}, e^{r_{observed_1}}, e^{r_{observed_2}}, e^{r_{shipped}} \right\} \tag{6.2}$$

$$E^C = \left\{ e^{C_{received}} \right\} \tag{6.3}$$

Referring to Amazon's Elastic Computing Cloud (EC2), 1 GB of network traffic from and to their EC2 costs between 0.06 EUR (0.08 USD) and 0.15 EUR (0.19 USD) depending on region and total amount of monthly traffic [7]. Thus, I assume average costs of 0.11 EUR (0.14 USD) per Gigabyte network traffic for operation of the service provider. Furthermore, I assume, every participant of a RFID-aided supply chain to perform authenticity checks during goods receipt, i.e. the amount of data that has to be validated using the service provider increases with the current position of the good in the supply chain.

On-Premise: An on-premise setup with the given supply chain configuration results in 2,472 byte of network traffic for counterfeit checks at the retailer's position p_4 as defined in Eq. 6.4. I developed Eq. 6.5 that defines the total network traffic c of all supply chain parties required to fulfill authenticity checks using a service provider for a supply chain of length l to check p pharmaceutical goods. The total network traffic for anti-counterfeiting checks of a single product in an on-premise setup amounts to 5,028 byte. This equals approx. 231,552 products that can be checked per Gigabyte network traffic.

$$c_{p_i} = 40\,\text{byte} + (i-1)(40\,\text{byte} + 756\,\text{byte}) + 44\,\text{byte} \qquad (6.4)$$

$$c_{on-premise} = p\left((l-1)84\,\text{byte} + \frac{l}{2}(l-1)796\,\text{byte}\right) \qquad (6.5)$$

For the given supply chain configuration, with $l = 4$ and $p = 15$ billion pharmaceuticals on prescription per year, the total network traffic of a purely on-premise solution amounts to $c \approx 70,240\,\text{GB}$ respectively $\approx 7,726\,\text{EUR}$ costs for network traffic across the global supply chain per year.

On-Demand: When applying an on-demand setup to wholesalers and to the dedicated service provider for anti-counterfeiting, the charged network traffic is reduced compared to a purely on-premise setup. The amount of incoming and outgoing network traffic in a purely on-demand setup amounts to 84 byte for each supply chain party. The total network traffic for anti-counterfeiting checks for a single product in the given mixed configuration amounts to a total of 252 byte, which is approx. 95 % less than an equivalent on-premise setup.

Apart from both extremes, a purely on-premise and a purely on-demand setup, I expect mainly wholesalers to adopt a SaaS solution. In Fig. 6.1 both RFID infrastructure setup are compared: on the left the on-premise approach is given whereas on the right a mixed SaaS approach is depicted. For the SaaS setup, I assume the service provider for anti-counterfeiting to be provided also as an on-

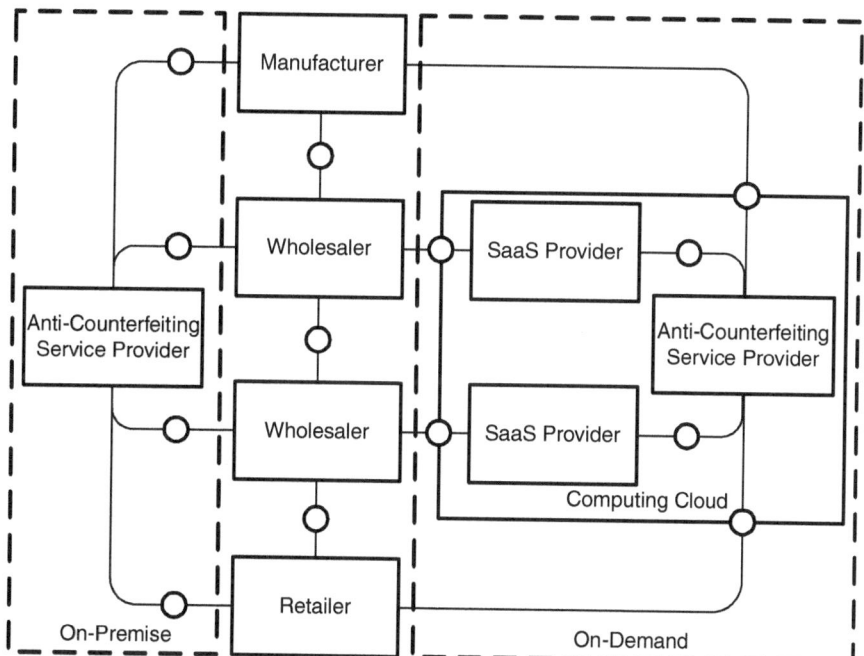

Fig. 6.1 Comparison of RFID setups: **a** On-premise, **b** On-demand

demand solution. Thus, the service provider is able to access EPCIS repositories of all supply chain participants directly using a SaaS solution. For example, a counterfeit check initiated by the retailer requires 880 byte of network traffic as defined by Eq. 6.6. This equals approx. 35 % of the network traffic required for authenticity check per product compared to an on-premise setup with 2,472 byte for the retailer role as defined by Eq. 6.4 for $l = 4$.

$$40 \, \text{byte} + 40 \, \text{byte} + 756 \, \text{byte} + 44 \, \text{byte} = 880 \, \text{byte} \qquad (6.6)$$

I enhanced Eq. 6.5 describing the total network traffic of a purely on-premise solution with supply chain length l for applicability in a SaaS solution. By integrating the assumption that network traffic within the provider's cloud or between providers of different clouds is less expensive or even free of charge [7]. Equation 6.8 extends Eq. 6.5 by subtracting the fraction of 796 byte network traffic for query and response of EPCIS repositories from the total network traffic. The impact is related to the party's position p_i within the supply chain taking the length of the supply chain l into account. The earlier the position of a supply chain party within a product's path incorporating a SaaS solution is, the later the impact of reduced network traffic. All supply chain parties with a higher position benefit from parties incorporating a SaaS solution.

The set S in Eq. 6.7 defines all supply chain participants, which make use of a SaaS solution. The parameter i defines the position of the participant p within the supply chain, i.e. the pharmaceutical manufacturer is defined by p_1 and the last participant of the supply chain by p_n.

$$S = \{p_1, \ldots, p_i, \ldots, p_n | i \in \mathbb{N}^+ \wedge p_i \text{ operates an on-demand solution}\} \qquad (6.7)$$

$$c_{combined} = p\left((l-1)84 \, \text{byte} + \left(\frac{l}{2}(l-1) - \sum_{i \in S}(l-i) \right) 796 \, \text{byte} \right) \qquad (6.8)$$

The concrete configuration for an on-demand and an on-premise setup is depicted in Fig. 6.1. For a combined on-demand and on-premise setup $S = \{2, 3\}$ and $l = 4$ are applied to the given pharmaceutical as introduced in Sect. 1.1. The network traffic is defined by Eq. 6.8 and amounts to $2,640$ byte per product or $c_{combined} \approx 36,880$ GB per year [8]. For a purely on-premise setup, the network traffic is defined by Eq. 6.5 and amounts to $c_{on-premise} \approx 70,240$ GB. The annual network costs for the entire supply chain are approx. 4,057 EUR for a combined on-demand and on-premise setup in contrast to 7,726 EUR for a purely on-premise setup [3]. This shows that the use of a combined on-demand and on-premise approach instead of a purely on-premise setup reduces initial investments for RFID-enablement with respect to SMEs, supports the migration towards an RFID-aided supply chain by reducing integration efforts, and optimized operational costs for network traffic by up to fifty percent.

References

1. M. Feldhofer, S. Dominikus, J. Wolkerstorfer, Strong authentication for RFID systems using the AES algorithm, in *Proceedings of the 6th International Workshop on Cryptographic Hardware and Embedded Systems* (2004), pp. 357–370
2. Global standards 1: EPCIS standard 1.0.1 (2007), http://www.gs1.org/gsmp/kc/epcglobal/epcis/epcis_1_0_1-standard-20070921.pdf. Accessed 8 Mar 2012
3. M.-P. Schapranow, M. Nagora, A. Zeier, CoMoSeR: cost model for security-enhanced RFID-aided supply chains, in *Proceedings of the 18th International Conference on Software Telecommunications and Computer Networks*, IEEE, 2010
4. Global standards 1: Preise für die Nutzung des Leistungspaketes GS1 complete (2011), http://www.gs1-germany.de/service/gs1_complete/preisliste/index_ger.html. Accessed 8 Mar 2012
5. M.-P. Schapranow, J. Müller, A. Zeier, H. Plattner, RFID event data processing: an architecture for storing and searching, in *Proceedings of the 4th International Workshop on RFID Technology: Concepts, Applications, Challenges*, 2010
6. J.F. Kurose, K.W. Ross, *Computer Networking: A Top-Down Approach*, 5th edn. (Addison-Wesley, Boston, 2009)
7. Amazon web services LLC, Pricing (2010), http://aws.amazon.com/ec2/pricing/. Accessed 8 Mar 2012
8. J. Müller et al., A simulation of the pharmaceutical supply chain to provide realistic test data, in *Proceedings of 1st International Conference on Advances in System Simulation*, IEEE, 2009

Chapter 7
Evaluation

In the following, I evaluate my contributions with respect to the pharmaceutical supply chain. In addition, their applicability to further industries is evaluated. As a result, my specific research results are evaluated from a holistic point of view and the social relevance of my contributions is underlined.

7.1 Applicability to Further Industries

This section provides a broader perspective of this contribution and its applicability. I abstract from the concrete pharmaceutical scenario given in Sect. 1.1 to discuss the applicability of my developed security extensions in context of further industries. Table 7.1 gives an empirical evaluation of this work's applicability to industries specified by the International Standard Industrial Classification (ISIC) defined by the United Nations [1]. The relevance column is classified by the author's opinion and builds on personal empirical experiences. Table 7.2 provides a list of personal constraints for industries, which focuses on the kind of handled goods, the potentials for product counterfeits and its impacts. Each industry of the ISIC is assigned to one or multiple constraints given in Table 7.2 to indicate the applicability of my work.

I consider constraints C4 and C5 as indicators for industries that suffer from a high rate of counterfeits. The remaining classes indicate criteria, which do not allow introduction of counterfeits or prevent the use of EPCglobal components for anti-counterfeiting. For example, constraint C1 considers closed supply chain, which makes it impossible for external suppliers to participate.

As a result of the constraint classification, ISIC classes A, C and G need to be considered as potential targets with the risk of counterfeit activities due to the handled goods and the supply chain structure. In the following, I discuss selected industry examples, which might benefit from the use of HBAC.

Matthieu-P. Schapranow, *Real-time Security Extensions for EPCglobal Networks*,
In-Memory Data Management Research, DOI: 10.1007/978-3-642-36343-6_7,
© Springer-Verlag Berlin Heidelberg 2014

Table 7.1 Empiric evaluation of applicability of security extensions to industries classes

ISIC	Description	Aff.	Constr.
A	Agriculture, forestry and fishing	H	C4
B	Mining and quarrying	N	C1,2
C	Manufacturing	H	C4,5
D	Electricity, gas, steam and air conditioning supply	N	C1,2,7
E	Water supply; sewerage, waste management and remediation activities	N	C2,7
F	Construction	N	C6
G	Wholesale and retail trade; repair of motor vehicles and motorcycles	H	C4,5
H	Transportation and storage	N	C6,7
I	Accommodation and food service activities	N	C6
J	Information and communication	N	C3,6
K	Financial and insurance activities	N	C3,6,8
L	Real estate activities	N	C6,8
M	Professional, scientific and technical activities	L	C6
N	Administrative and support service activities	N	C6
O	Public administration and defense; compulsory social security	L	C3,6
P	Education	N	C6
Q	Human health and social work activities	H	C6,7
R	Arts, entertainment and recreation	L	C6,8
S	Other service activities	N	C6
T	Activities of households as employers; undifferentiated goods- and services- producing activities of households for own use	N	C3,6
U	Activities of extraterritorial organizations and bodies	N	C6

Aff. Affinity, *Constr.* Constraints, *H* High, *L* Low, *N* None

Table 7.2 Evaluation constraints for industries based on empiric categories

Cat.	Constraint description
C1	Closed supply chain, i.e. restrictions to enter the market exist
C2	A relatively fixed number of participants within the supply chain
C3	Missing use of product ingredients
C4	Use of standardized ingredients supplied by various vendors
C5	Supply relationships are considered as sensitive information
C6	Service sector misses traceable products; service is the product
C7	Goods cannot be tracked individually
C8	Only unique products are exchanged, thus they cannot be exchanged

Retail Trading Industries

Due to standardization, product characteristics, such as weight, ingredients, functionalities, etc., are precisely defined. Standardization enables multiple vendors to manufacture products following certain specifications while leaving the internals open to their specific design. As a result, comparable products of different vendors become interchangeable. Formally, products become functions with a clearly defined reaction to a set of input values. On the one hand, the opportunity to switch vendors reduces dependability on a certain supplier. On the other hand, vendors are forced to optimize manufacturing costs since cheaper products are more likely to be chosen. I consider high costs of competitors' products as a potential entry point for cheap counterfeiters [2, Sect. 2.3].

With reference to the motivation of this work, standardization is present in the pharmaceutical industry. Medicines with equivalent ingredients are referred to as multi-source pharmaceuticals or generic pharmaceuticals [3, Sect. 12]. Pharmaceuticals are part of a global retail market. The following list depicts a brief selection of industries and products suffering from counterfeits [4]:

- **Pharmaceuticals:** Party drugs, Viagra, etc.,
- **Cloths:** Brand name clothes, luggage, leather articles, shirts, suites, etc.,
- **Entertainment Electronics:** Telephones, discs, computers, etc., and
- **Spare Parts:** Car accessories (breaks), aircraft components (tires), electronic equipment (batteries), etc.

It exemplarily shows the variety of industries that already suffer from or may suffer in future from product counterfeits [2, Sect. 4.1]. Products of the given examples are exchanged via more or less open supply chains. Tracking individual goods with the help of EPCglobal networks should be considered to verify the product's authenticity. I consider EPCglobal networks as an additional market restriction for counterfeiters that prevents injection of faked products into open supply chains. The need for security extensions in this context arises from the wish to automatically exchange product-relevant data with known and unknown business partners without exposing confidential business internals as described in Sect. 3.1.

Human Health Industries

In a cooperation project with the Charité—Universitätsmedizin Berlin, I was confronted with data security and privacy aspects of medical records. The following groups of employees are working at Charité: medical doctors treating patients and medical researchers deriving new scientific knowledge. Personalized medicine requires various departments to perform analysis on patient samples, e.g. blood, tissue, biopsy, etc. to generate more and more fine-grained results. Specialized departments generate the latter with limited knowledge of the actual patient. The combination of the analysis by medical doctors is an essential source of information for decision taking, e.g. to select appropriate medical treatments. Each of the individual medical processes results in data processed by IT systems across various clinical departments. A centralized access control is preferable to minimize administrative overhead and to guarantee a holistic and consistent view on patient data.

In the course of the cooperation project, I contributed to the iPad application Oncolyzer. It provides medical doctors and researchers with all relevant tumor data of a certain patient. It combines data from various data sources and departments in real-time. In addition, in-memory technology supports researchers by providing flexible real-time analysis of patient cohorts on the iPad. This supports the war on cancer disease by reducing the time to identify and combine relevant data.

From the data protection's perspective, sensitive patient data displayed on the iPad must be protected. As a result, access control is an essential aspect of preventing data leakage. In addition to existing user authentication based on username and password, the presented HBAC ensures that combinations of sensitive data are only accessible by authorized personnel while they are involved in the treatment process. The existing user authentication is used for identification of users accessing the application. Due to the defined access rules, medical doctors are able to see detailed information of patients to treat. In contrast, medical researchers do not need to access all patient data for their work, e.g. to perform statistical analysis. As a result, aggregations of fine-grained data reduce its granularity, e.g. to prevent patient profiling. Since medical researchers are also involved in the treatment process of certain patient cohorts, e.g. for clinical studies, they have limited access to fine-grained patient data. HBAC can be used to prevent the exposure of fine-grained patient data by monitoring the complete query history. The transparent design of HBAC reduces integration efforts within existing IT infrastructures. Thus, there is no need for code modifications of the Oncolyzer iPad application. Sensitive data are filtered and replaced by default values by the security extensions instantly during data exchange. The business-level security extension requires a specific filter for the exchanged data format: in this case the human readable JavaScript Object Notation (JSON).

This example shows, how access to sensitive data can be controlled without the need for concrete control on per-user basis. The transparent design of the security extensions supports the integration process within existing IT landscapes and reduces setup efforts.

Energy Supplying Industries

In the course of my research work, I was also confronted with challenges of data processing in smart grids. I refer to a *smart grid* as an energy network that can react to actions of different users, e.g. suppliers or consumers. In a smart grid, households are equipped with smart meters, which record the energy consumption in intervals and can be read-out remotely [5]. From a data protection point of view, meter readings need to be considered as sensitive data. By acquiring meter readings, attacker can derive customer profiles including individual working hours, holiday times, and the presence of characteristic devices in the household. The EC currently investigates the data protection aspect in smart grids. For example, the working party recommends the prevention of unauthorized disclosure of personal data, guaranteed data integrity, appropriate access control and aggregation of smart metering data whenever appropriate [6].

HBAC can be applied to smart grids for improving protection of sensitive metering data as recommended by the EC. Metering data can be automatically exchanged while individual access rules specified by customers that control access to personal meter readings. Access rules are used by HBAC to prevent combination of meter readings with external data, such as location-based data. In other words, HBAC prevents the combination of metering data to derive customer profiles depending on the receiver's business role. Furthermore, it enforces the principle of data minimalism [7]. Thus, certain business partners, e.g. energy suppliers, analytical service providers, etc., only receive the portion of data in the granularity that is relevant for their tasks. Since most of the attack scenarios for smart grids require access to fine-grained metering data, a higher level of data granularity eliminates these attacks. For example, exchanging aggregated consumption readings on a daily or a weekly basis instead of as fine-grained 15-min intervals of metering data impeded the derivation of customer in-house times since peak times cannot be detected. The presented access control mechanisms also raise flexibility in applying access decision. In contrast to existing access control mechanisms that support only bivalent decision taking, HBAC enables the use of a continuous spectrum of access decision. For example, metering data are only available during a certain time window of the day, e.g. from 8 p.m. to 8 a.m., to prevent surveillance of inhabitants living in a flat or house.

7.2 Impact on Business Processes

I evaluate the impact of the presented security extensions on existing business processes in the following. The aspects of migrating towards security extensions and their regular usage are considered.

Migration Phase: The migration to a security standard or a new IT system is also challenging for IT experts since productive environments cannot be replaced instantly. Thus, the productive IT environment is modeled in certain test or laboratory environments where updates and changes can be tested before migrating productive systems. For productive environments the planned downtime for upgrades is considered as the key indicator of the complexity and the feasibility of a migration to new software or release. From a business point of view, the downtime needs to be minimized and must not exceed business closing times, e.g. weekends. However, for certain 24/7 manufacturing industries, such as pharmaceutical manufacturers, even a downtime of two days during weekends is not acceptable. Thus, certain updates cannot be processed due to the need for data migration that takes multiple days or weeks.

From a system's engineering point of view, the migration process needs to be considered during the design phase of the new IT component. Keeping the requirements of future business users in mind supports its adaption. I consider the migration to security extensions as a critical factor for upgrading enterprise systems. Thus, I focused on developing transparent security extensions that can be enabled in parallel to existing IT systems without the need for an interruption. As a result, a second IT landscape incorporating the security extensions can be established step-by-step while the current IT landscape remains unchanged. A step-wise switch towards security extensions can be performed and the new landscape can be tested and verified. Once security extensions are fully installed and configured to support the existing EPCIS repository, the existing landscape without security extensions can be turned down to restrict access via security extensions only. The transparent design of the security extensions addresses the non-functional requirement N4 defined in Sect. 3.1.3. It does not involve any kind of time-consuming data migration and the EPCIS configuration remains unchanged. I consider the transparent integration of security extensions as the basis for a high adoption rate. In contrast to traditional upgrade processes, which result in down-time, the outlined side-by-side integration eliminates the need for downtime of existing IT systems. As a result, involved business processes are not affected during migration phase.

Regular Usage: The regular use of security extensions has the major aim to reduce the risk of data attacks and to prevent exposure of sensitive business secrets. From a system engineering point of view, the required infrastructure components as part of the security extension discussed in Chap. 5 need to be installed and configured once. Afterwards, the only difference in existing business processes is that data communications are adapted to use the enhanced communication protocol via a secured channel instead of the unsecured one. In addition, the ACC software component needs to be installed and supervised to work on the client site.

From a business point of view, the analysis of tracking data needs to be inte-grated into existing business process. For example, querying an anti-counterfeiting service provider needs to be implemented by pharmaceutical wholesalers or pharmacies to check product authenticity. I consider adaption of existing business processes as tasks that are part of the RFID-enablement process and not as part of migration towards the given security extensions.

From the application's perspective, there is no difference if the security extensions do not detect any violated access rule since event data pass without any modifications. If there is a need for adapting filtering the result set is required. All applications that process event data work with the only difference that filtered values are replaced by default values or empty values instead of its sensitive pendant.

The presented security extensions were designed with transparency in mind. As a result, existing business processes are only minimally affected. From a technical point of view, a one-time installation of the required software components is the major effort.

7.3 Social Relevance

Ultimately, I discuss the many-folded relevance of my contributions. The estab-lishment of data protection is a challenging task since it is rarely considered during the design of IT systems. As a result, the IT system is already in place when considerations about IT security arise, e.g. due to a concrete hacker attack. The title of the work stresses this fact, since I focus on security extensions and not security mechanisms only. The given dissertation has shown how to apply security mechanisms in a transparent way to existing IT systems focusing on components of EPCglobal networks. Thus, existing IT systems do not need to be modified. The chosen design approach supports its fast adoption. Therefore, increased data security in EPCglobal networks within companies and between business partners can be applied with minimal efforts and downtimes.

The depicted pharmaceutical scenario showed the impact of counterfeits. Furthermore, it showed the still open liability issue in context of faked medicines. A reliable process for verification of the product's authenticity enables all supply chain participants to distinguish between authentic and faked products. As a result, the future introduction of a dedicated service provider for anti-counterfeiting shifts liability for detecting and removing counterfeits from manufacturers to all supply chain parties handling a certain product. My contribution supports the future introduction of a service provider in EPCglobal networks by providing a reliable basis for exchanging confidential event data in vulnerable environments while keeping business secrets closed.

With respect to Hyp. 1 the response time of the developed security extensions is valued as the major acceptance criteria for industry-wide usage. The conducted benchmarks showed promising results for response time results to meet this hypothesis.

For identification and authentication of involved supply chain parties a PKI was integrated in the architecture of the security extension. Nowadays, a central PKI for identification purposes in supply chains exists neither on a national nor on an international basis. However, the experience of national projects exist and can be reapplied to this concrete application scenario, e.g. the introduction of a PKI for the electronic identity card in Germany [8]. With respect to Hyp. 2 certificate identifiers are stored within the in-memory database of the ACS. They are used for identification of inquirers, which forms the basis for authentication within the security extensions.

Furthermore, my designed IT artifact with respect to the design science methodology showed that the ACS successfully manages individual shared keys per user for specific encryption of event data. The fine-grained key management approach was chosen with respect to Hyp. 3. On the one hand, it comes with an additional key management overhead. On the other hand, it enables revocation of encryption keys for specific users. Thus, the impact of key exposure is drastically reduced in context of the presented security extensions. In contrast to a single shared key that is used for encryption of data for all parties, the use of individual keys per user enables individual revocation. Moreover, regular updates of the individual encryption key limit the amount of data that can be decrypted by an attacker that obtained a valid key.

As a result, I value EPCglobal networks incorporating additional security extensions as a valid foundation of protection of fast-moving consumer goods, such as pharmaceuticals, without significantly delaying existing business processes, such as goods receipt and goods shipment. As a result, EPCglobal networks also provide a competitive advantage in goods processing.

The presented contributions are not limited to EPCglobal networks and its use in the pharmaceutical industry in combination with RFID technology. Moreover, it can be applied to further industries and scenarios in a world driven by increased globalization as described in Sect. 7.1. The social aspect of my contributions can be broadened to industries that suffer from counterfeits and for use with other tracking and tracing technologies, such as two-dimensional barcodes or data matrices. Further approaches for protection of goods, such as optical marking, holograms, watermarks, etc. can be found in related work [9, Sect. 6.2]. Introducing any kind of fine-grained tracking and tracing technology on item level is the key-enabler for unique product identification. However, the more fine-grained the tracking data are, the higher is the risk of customer profiling and exposure of business secrets.

I stress the use of fine-grained tracking and tracing techniques for protection of products as an additional aspect of the social relevance of my work. I showed that transforming the current pharmaceutical supply chains towards an RFID-aided supply chain, for example, could be amortized by less than ten percent of product surcharges within a timeframe of five years. This underlines two aspects. Firstly, it underlines the applicability of RFID technology to enable automatic anti-counterfeiting. Secondly, it shows that operating costs of a service provider for anti-counterfeiting are driven by the network costs for exchanging event data.

Moreover, I stress the social relevance of my contribution for applications running on mobile devices. The variety of devices, services, and user accounts makes it hard to identify users beyond borders of devices and IT systems. Although various open approaches, such as openID, exist, there is no single point of truth for meta identification of users [10]. However, with the help of HBAC the combination of behavioral observation data with queries results in criteria for controlling access of individual users to a variety of systems.

In other words, next generation identification can be formally considered as a function that incorporates various kinds of sensors as input values and adapts access rights specifically depending on the analyzed behavior, e.g. history of queries and actions. I consider an adaptive access control mechanisms, such as HBAC, as a possible basis for implementing next generation identity.

References

1. United Nations, International Standard Industrial Classification of All Economic Activities Rev. 4. Technical Report 4, Department of Economic and Social Affairs, 2008
2. Ernst & Young, Piraten des 21. Jahrhunderts—Angriff auf die Konsumgüterindustrie (2008), http://www.markenverband.de/publikationen/studien/StudievonErnst-YoungPiratendes21.Jahr hunderts.pdf. Accessed 8 Mar 2012
3. World Health Organization, WHO Expert Committee on Specifications for Pharmaceutical Preparations. Technical Report 929, World Health Organization, 2005
4. R. Fe, *The Economic Impact of Counterfeiting and Piracy* (Organisation for Economic Co-operation and Development, Paris, 2008)

5. M.-P. Schapranow, R. Kühne, A. Zeier, Enabling real-time charging for smart grid infrastructures using in-memory databases, in *Proceedings of the 1st Workshop on Smart Grid Networking Infrastructure*, 2010
6. Data Protection Working Party, Opinion 12/2011 on Smart Metering (2011), http://idpc.gov.mt/dbfile.aspx/WP_183.pdf. Accessed 8 Mar 2012
7. Federal Office for Information Security, BSI Standard 100-1: Information Security Management, System V. 1.5, 2008
8. Bundesamt für Sicherheit in der Informationstechnik, BSI TR-03128 EAC-PKI'n für den elektronischen Personalausweis, V. 1.1. (2010), https://www.bsi.bund.de/ContentBSI/Publikationen/TechnischeRichtlinien/tr03128/index_htm.html. Accessed 8 Mar 2012
9. IMPACT Secretariat at AIFA (ed.) *IMPACT—The Handbook* (International Medical Products Anti-Counterfeiting Taskforce, Geneva, 2011)
10. J. Bellamy-McIntyre, C. Luterroth, G. Weber, OpenID and the Enterprise: a model-based analysis of single sign-on authentication, in *Proceedings of 15th International Enterprise Distributed Object Computing Conference*, Los Alamitos, CA, USA. IEEE Computer Society, 2011, pp. 129–138

Chapter 8
Conclusion

The given dissertation contains the results of my research work in the fields of EPCglobal networks, access control mechanisms, and in-memory technology. In the course of my work, I was inspired by various discussions about complex enterprise systems. One of the challenging aspects of the increasing use of IT systems in supply chain management is the fact that more and more fine-grained enterprise data are captured and need to be processed in an automated manner. Data processing needs to be performed in real-time, e.g. to improve goods receipt or goods shipment. Anti-counterfeiting techniques in the pharmaceutical supply chain drive the motivation of my research activities since pharmaceutical counterfeits potentially harm or even kill human beings. I consider protecting human life from pharmaceuticals with inappropriate ingredients as the social motivation of my work. The analysis of related work and EPCglobal definitions showed an insufficient consideration of data protection aspects within EPCglobal networks. As a result, the given work analyzes specific attacks for EPCglobal networks and evaluates their business impacts. Thus, I considered device-level and business-level security extensions.

From the device-level perspective, RFID tags are one technical basis for tracking and tracing of goods. Mutual authentication protocols for passive RFID tags are one possible extension of device-level security. The use of RFID tags is a concrete technical assumption, but further tracking and tracing techniques exist, e.g. data matrix, holograms. My analysis of related work showed that extensions for business-level security are rarely considered. This has created the motivation to engineer a concrete transparent measure to protect EPCglobal components. I consider fine-grained product meta data as sensitive business secrets in EPCglobal networks, which can be misused to derive company-specific knowledge. This work contributes by enhancing data security in EPCglobal networks. It shows a proof-of-concept for a secured tracking and tracing scenario for the pharmaceutical industry. I showed that security extensions for EPCglobal networks could improve data protection of product meta data. Furthermore, this work introduces a transparent software design that minimizes the integration efforts. The developed access control mechanisms define a new understanding of control. In contrast to

Matthieu-P. Schapranow, *Real-time Security Extensions for EPCglobal Networks*,
In-Memory Data Management Research, DOI: 10.1007/978-3-642-36343-6_8,
© Springer-Verlag Berlin Heidelberg 2014

traditional access control mechanisms that either grant or decline access to a certain resource in a bivalent way, the given access control mechanisms are able to grant access within an interval from complete grant to complete decline. This continuous spectrum of control supports the inquirer, who receives always a semantically valid result set, and the owner of event data, who is able to decide, which portion of data to exchange. Access decisions are taken at the latest point in time just before data is returned to the querying application. The late enforcement of access rights embarks data leakages by revoking access rights, which results in ad-hoc prevention of further data leakage. The usage of a PKI enables identification of business partners and reconstruction of attack paths.

The key-enabler for performing HBAC analysis in real-time is the in-memory technology. From the storage's perspective, keeping the complete history of queries is a challenging task. Performing real-time analysis on top of the entire history is an analytical challenge. In-memory technology addresses both requirements. Partitioning data across multiple blade systems and parallel processing of queries reduce the overall response time below the empirical threshold of two seconds. In addition, the columnar database layout supports the use of lightweight compression techniques to store the history in a compressed format. As a result, the storage demands for storing the complete history are reduced while the efficiency of data processing is improved.

With the help of the benchmark results, I verified the applicability of my developed security extensions for EPCglobal networks for an industrial real-world use. Furthermore, the results have proved my research hypothesis, which stated that security extensions should not delay existing business processes significantly. However, the current database layout of the ACS is designed to fit for traditional and in-memory databases equally. Since the benchmark results proved the in-memory database to perform better, an optimized database layout is left open for further research. Designing a de-normalized database schema for the incorporated in-memory databases would result in less join operations and might improve response time additionally.

From the system engineering's perspective, I performed a qualitative and quantitative discussion of RFID-aided supply chains as technology basis for EPCglobal networks. I showed that an amortization of initial investments for RFID-enablement of the pharmaceutical supply chain is possible by moderate product surcharges within a timeframe of five years. Other tracking and tracing technologies, such as two-dimensional barcodes, are also applicable. The evaluation of the research results showed that HBAC could also be applied to further industries and business scenarios, e.g. to protect sensitive patient data in hospitals or fine-grained metering data in smart grids. I do not want to limit the applicability of my research results to a concrete research area or industry. In contrast, I want to indicate the broader applicability of the research results.

With developing tag capabilities, competitive advantages of RFID-aided supply chains will dominate. For example, active RFID tags will provide sensor data or location-based information. Their continuous integration in business processes forms the basis for gapless monitoring of goods and ingredients inside the supply chain. Individual supply chain parties will have specific access rights to gather specific product meta data relevant for their tasks. From my perspective, supply chains will converge to complex decentralized IT systems placed in a vulnerable environment with the need to interact with hundreds of thousands of users, sensors, and goods.

I motivate the interested reader to use the understanding of the presented concepts and concrete examples as a basis to identify further business scenarios, where the presented security extensions are applicable.

Appendices

The following sections represent the appendices of my dissertation. They containadditional details, which are referenced in my work.

A.1 Classification of Related Work

The following section contains the detailed classification of related work, which builds the basis for the evaluation in Chap. 2. Abbreviations used for classification are defined in Table A.1.

Table A.1 Abbreviations for classification of related work

Abbreviation	Description
A	Air Interface
D	EPC Discovery Service
H	Hardware
L	Location-based Services
M	Middleware
O	Object Naming Service
R	EPCIS Repository
S	Software
T	RFID Tag
Z	Summary

Table A.2 Classification of related work: access control fundamentals (abbreviations see Table A.1)

Year	Author	Concepts	Type	Auth.	AC	Comp.	XML
1971	Lampson [1]	✔		S		✔	
1992	Ferraiolo and Kuhn [2]	✔					✔
1998	Edjlila [3]		S		✔	Java Code	
2003	Abadi and Fournet [4]		S		✔	Program Code	

Matthieu-P. Schapranow, *Real-time Security Extensions for EPCglobal Networks*,
In-Memory Data Management Research, DOI: 10.1007/978-3-642-36343-6,
© Springer-Verlag Berlin Heidelberg 2014

Table A.3 Classification of related work: RFID-specifics 2005 (abbreviations see Table A.1)

Author	Concepts	Threats	Type	Auth.	AC	Comp.	XML	ISIC	Enc.
Günther and Spiekermann [5]	✓	✓							
Garfinkel et al. [6]	✓	✓	Z			A, T			
Song et al. [7]			S	✓	✓				

Table A.4 Classification of related work: RFID-specifics 2006 (abbreviations see Table A.1)

Author	Concepts	Threats	Type	Auth.	AC	Comp.	XML	ISIC	Enc.
Yagüe [8]			S, Z	✓			✓		
Hu et al. [9]	✓		S	✓					
Rieback et al. [10]		✓	H	✓	✓	A			
Rieback et al. [11]	✓	✓		✓	✓	A, T		✓	
Juels [12]	✓	✓	H, S			A, T			✓
Kim and Kim [13]			S	✓		M	✓		
Peris-Lopez et al. [14]	✓	✓				A, T			

Table A.5 Classification of related work: RFID-specifics 2007 (abbreviations see Table A.1)

Author	Concepts	Threats	Type	Auth.	AC	Comp.	XML	ISIC	Enc.
Grummt et al. [15]	✓				✓	R, D	✓		
Groba et al. [16]			S		✓	L	✓		
King and Zhang [17]			S	✓		A, T		Q	✓
Fabian and Günther [18]		✓	S		✓	O			✓
Evdokimo and Günther [19]			S		✓	R			✓
Ilic et al. [20]			S		✓	T		Q	
Langheinrich [21]	✓	✓	Z	✓	✓			K	

Table A.6 Classification of related work: RFID-specifics 2008 (abbreviations see Table A.1)

Author	Concepts	Threats	Type	Auth.	AC	Comp.	XML	ISIC	Enc.
Grummt and Müller [22]			S		✓	R	✓		
Grummt and Schöffel [23]			S		✓	R	✓		
Rotter [24]	✓	✓			✓	T			
Sheng et al. [25]	✓	✓				M, R		G, H	
Chung et al. [26]			S	✓	✓				

Table A.7 Classification of related work: RFID-specifics 2009 (abbreviations see Table A.1)

Author	Concepts	Threats	Type	Auth.	AC	Comp.	XML	ISIC	Enc.
Spiekermann and Evdokimov [27]	✓			✓		A			
Grummt and Schill [28]			S	✓	✓	R	✓	G	
Fabian and Günther [29]		✓	S			O			
Du et al. [30]			S		✓	M	✓		
Ilic et al. [31]			S			E		A, Q	
Xia and Han [32]		✓	S	✓		A, T			✓

A.2 Mapping for Discrete Event Simulation

The following section depicts the developed mapping of entities from EPCglobal networks and network simulator 3 entities and vice versa. This mapping is required for discrete event simulation as described in Sect. 3.2.2.

Table A.8 Mapping of entities of EPCglobal networks to network simulator and vice versa

Abstraction	EPCglobal network	Network simulator
Node	Supply chain participant, e.g. manufacturer, wholesaler, retailer	ns3::Node
In-/Output	Goods receiving/shipping area	ns3::P2PNetDevice
Link	Transportation route	ns3::P2PChannel
Entity handling unit	Freight vehicle, e.g. aircraft, ship, truck, container, pallet, packet, etc.	ns3::Packet

A.3 Authentication of Supply Chain Parties

The following section shows X.509 certificates used for authentication of supply chain parties in context of HBAC as described in Chap. 5.

Listing A.1. X.509: Excerpt of certificate for authentication of an ACC of a supply chain party, key length 2 kB

```
 1  Certificate:
 2      Data:
 3          Version: 3 (0x2)
 4          Serial Number: 9999 (0x270f)
 5          Signature Algorithm: sha1WithRSAEncryption
 6          Issuer: C=DE, ST=Brandenburg, L=Potsdam, O=HPI, OU=
                EPIC, CN=HBAC-CA
 7          Validity
 8              Not Before: Feb 20 07:32:58 2012 GMT
 9              Not After : Feb 19 07:32:58 2013 GMT
10          Subject: C=DE, CN=Pharma9999, L=Potsdam, O=HPI, ST=
                Brandenburg, OU=EPIC
11          Subject Public Key Info:
12              Public Key Algorithm: rsaEncryption
13              RSA Public Key: (2048 bit)
```

A.4 Enforcement of Access Rights

The following section depicts the developed mapping of operators and values between SOAP and ODRL messages and vice versa. This mapping is required for

Table A.9 Mapping to extract digital rights information from simple event query

Category	SOAP [33, Sect. 8.2.7.1]	↔	ODRL [34]
Values	param.name.MATCH_epc.value	↔	permission.asset.uid
	param.name = [SOAP Operator]_[attribute]	↔	permission.constraint.Operator = [ODRL Operator], permission.constraint.name = [attribute]
	param.value = 2010-10-04T00:00:00	↔	permission.constraint.rightOperand = 2010-10-04T00:00:00
Operators	GE	↔	gteq
	LT	↔	lt
	EQ	↔	eq

the extended communication protocol as described in Sect. 5.3. In addition, a request and response pair of SOAP and ODRL is exemplarily depicted. It builds the basis for enforcement of access rights in context of HBAC.

A.5 Benchmark Results

The following section contains detailed benchmark results, which are discussed in Sect. 5.7.2. The parameters for the approximation function of the form $rsp(l_h) = b \cdot l_h^d$ are given in Table A.10 for the individual benchmarks.

Table A.10 Comparison of benchmark setups in a multi-user environment with four clients querying 1,000 random queries in parallel

Setup	Policy	P	H	Inq.	b	d	MRT [s]	Figures
A	None	1	1	4	0.0001	0.6158	0.1914	A.1
B	None	1	1	10 k	0.0113	0.2168	0.1523	A.2
C	Ra	4	4	4	0.0007	0.5145	0.3625	A.3
D	RR	4	4	4	0.0003	0.5762	0.3613	A.4
E	Ra	4	4	10 k	0.1916	0.0434	0.3214	A.5
F	RR	4	4	10 k	0.1784	0.0496	0.3224	A.6
G	Ra	10	4	10 k	0.0831	0.1257	0.3738	A.7
H	RR	10	4	10 k	0.1799	0.0529	0.3381	A.8
I	Ra	100	4	10 k	0.0424	0.2037	0.4879	A.9
J	RR	100	4	10 k	0.0902	0.1355	0.4561	A.10
K	Ra + idx	100	4	10 k	0.0993	0.1231	0.4324	A.11
L	MySQL	1	1	10 k	0.7314	0.3422	19.1447	A.12

H Hosts, *MRT* Mean response time, *P* Partitions, *Ra* Range partitioning, *RR* Round robin partitioning

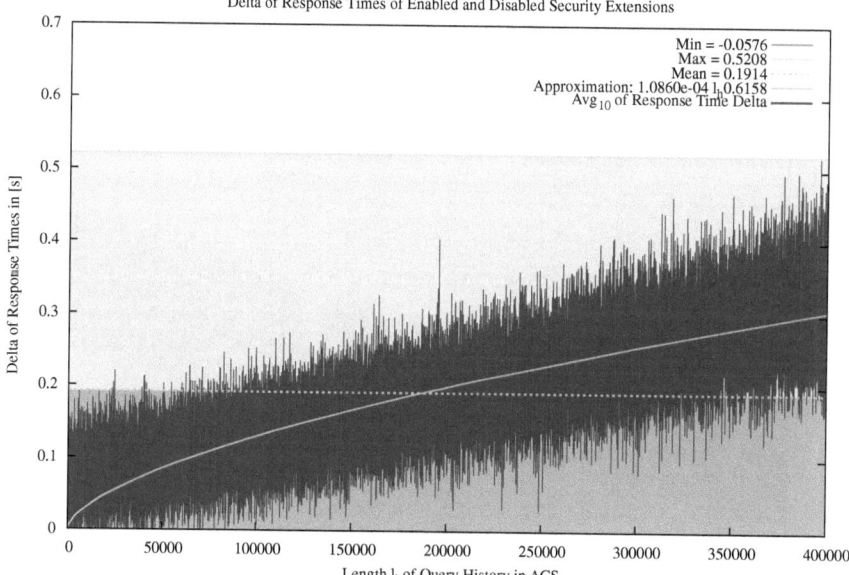

Fig. A.1 Delta of response times of FOSSTRAK capture client, 4 inquirers, no partitioning

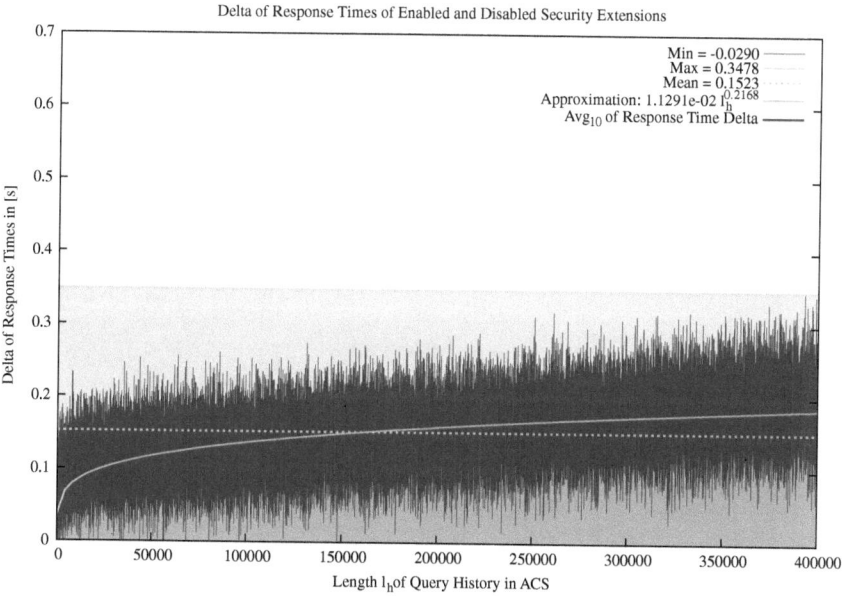

Fig. A.2 Delta of response times of FOSSTRAK capture client, 10 k inquirers, no partitioning

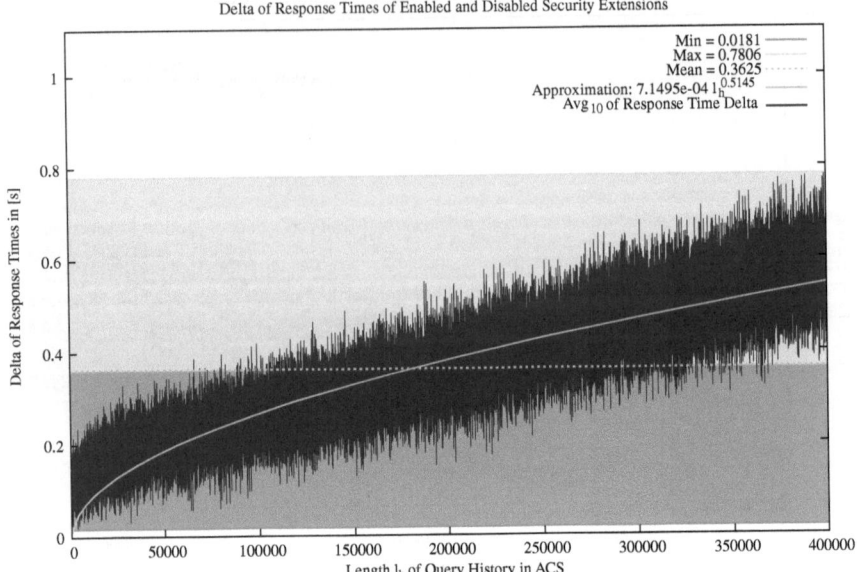

Fig. A.3 Delta of response times of FOSSTRAK capture client, 4 inquirers, RANGE 1, 2, 3, 4

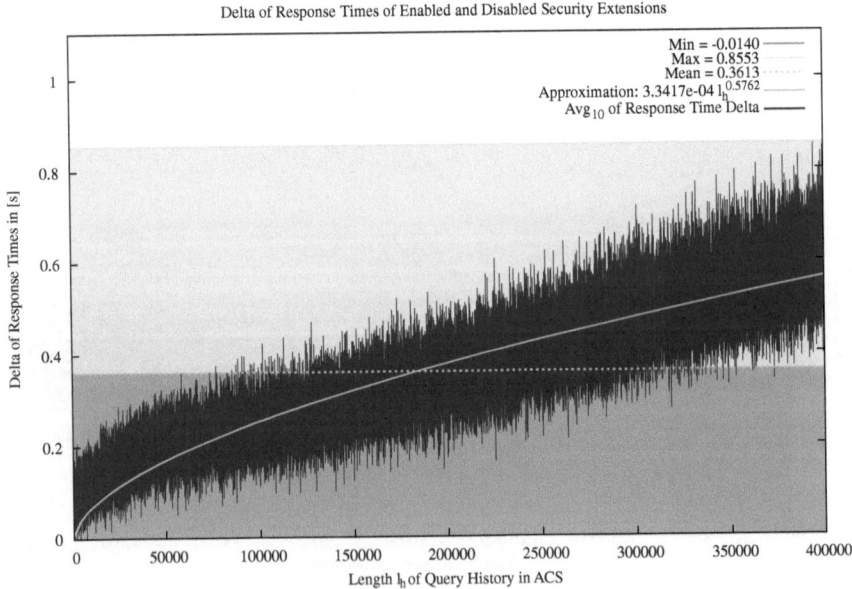

Fig. A.4 Delta of response times of FOSSTRAK capture client, 4 inquirers, ROUNDROBIN 4

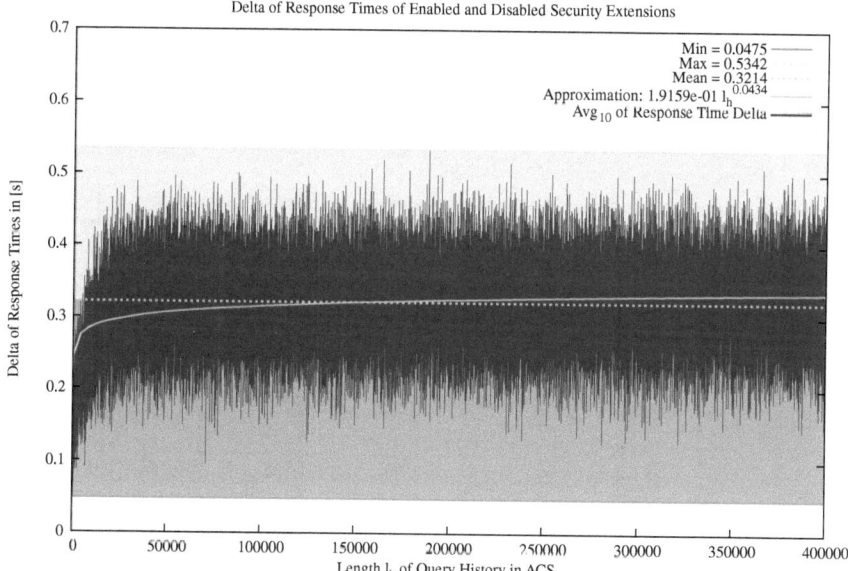

Fig. A.5 Delta of response times of FOSSTRAK capture client, 10 k inquirers, 4 range partitions

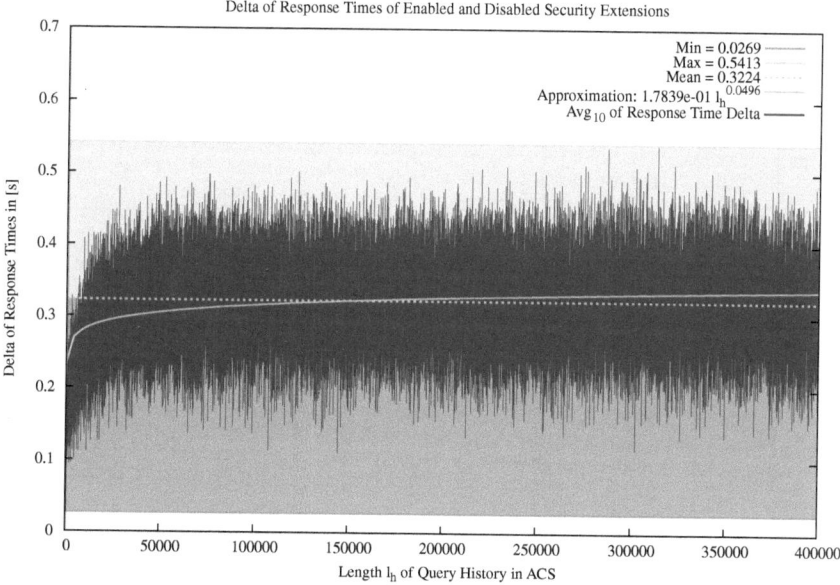

Fig. A.6 Delta of response times of FOSSTRAK capture client, 10 k inquirers, 4 round robin partitions

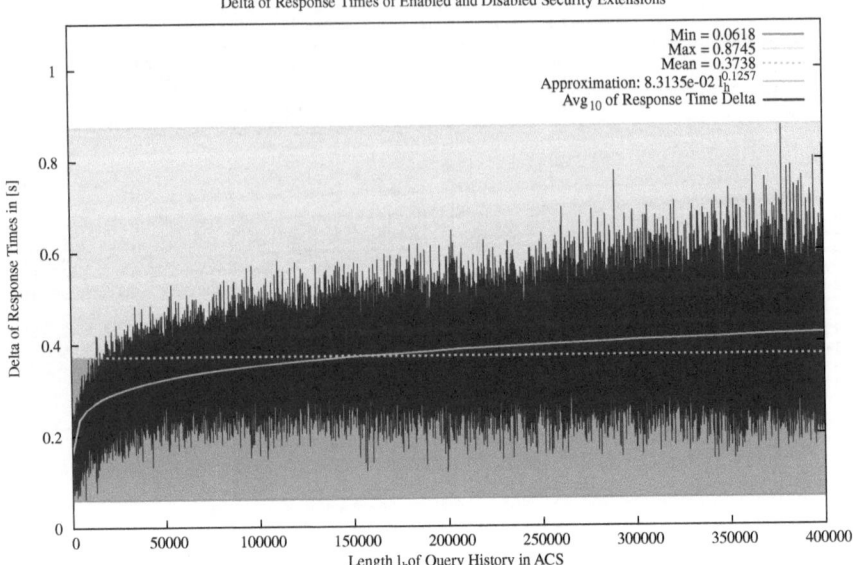

Fig. A.7 Delta of response times of FOSSTRAK capture client, 10 k inquirers, 10 range partitions

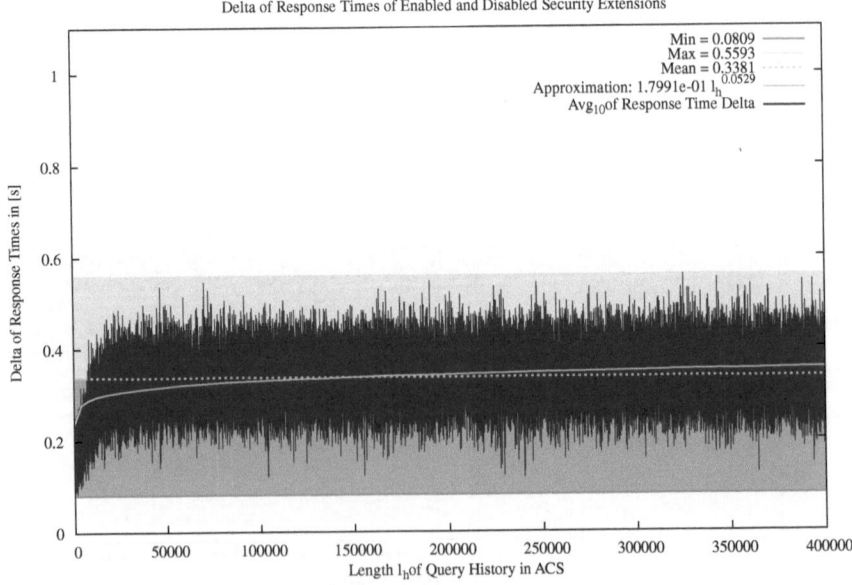

Fig. A.8 Delta of response times of FOSSTRAK capture client, 10 k inquirers, 10 round robin partitions

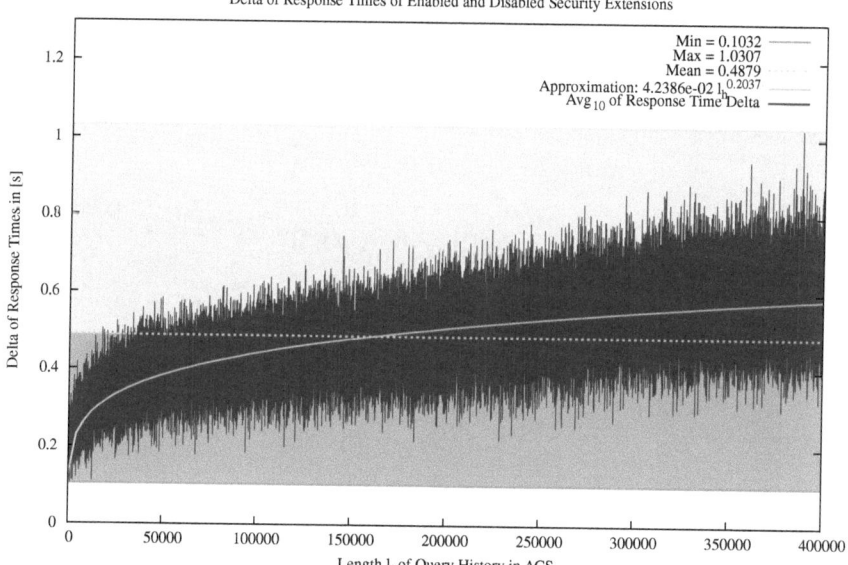

Fig. A.9 Delta of response times of FOSSTRAK capture client, 10 k inquirers, 100 range partitions

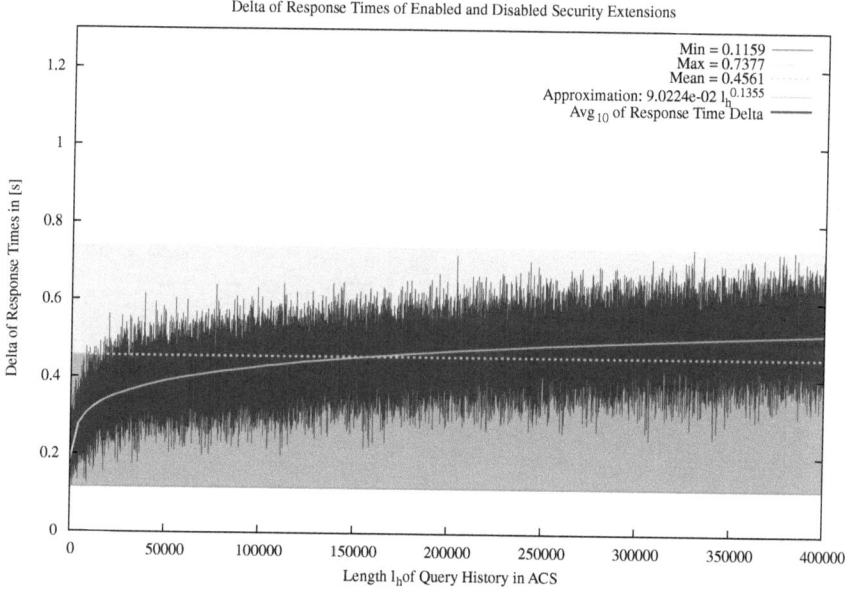

Fig. A.10 Delta of response times of FOSSTRAK capture client, 10 k inquirers, 100 round robin partitions

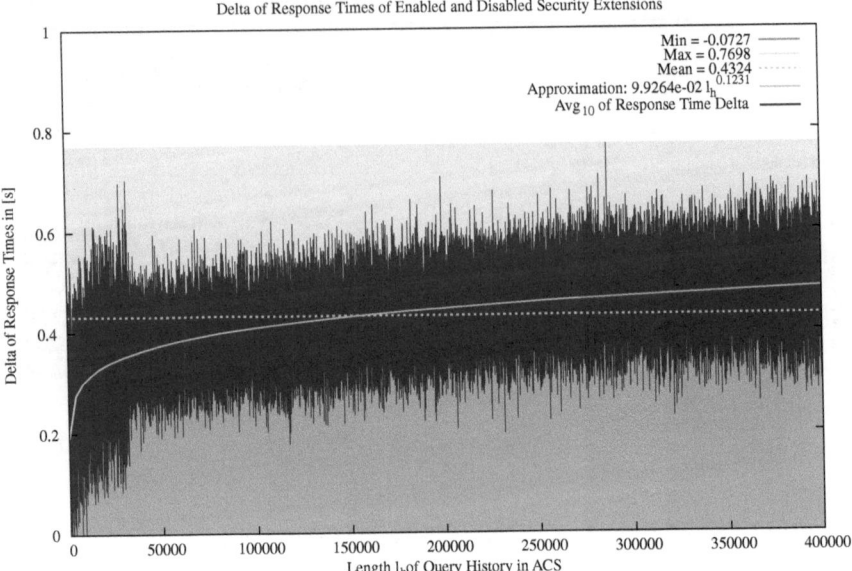

Fig. A.11 Delta of response times of FOSSTRAK capture client, 10 k inquirers, 100 range partitions, indexes on attributes identities and requests

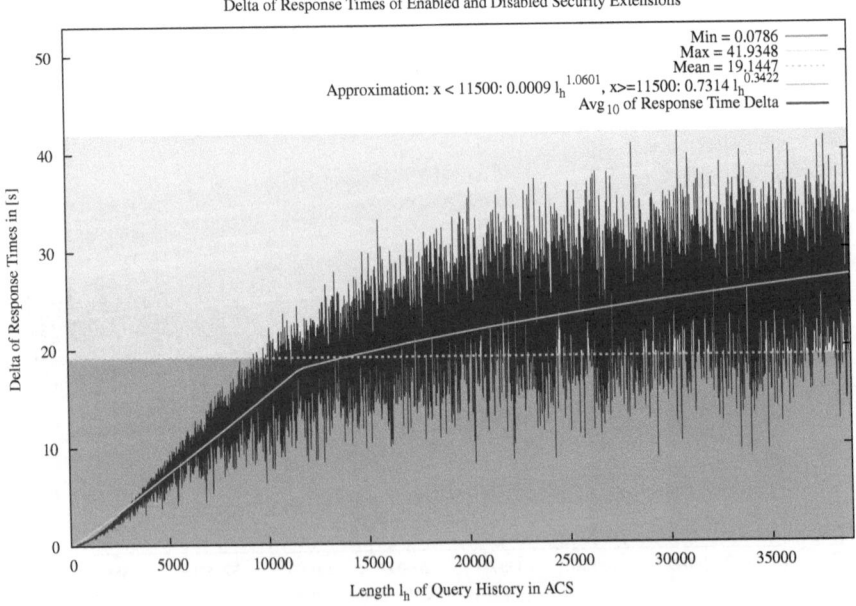

Fig. A.12 Delta of response times of FOSSTRAK capture client, 10 k inquirers, no partitioning, MySQL

Listing A.2 SOAP: Simple event query for filtered event data within a certain event time frame only with action observe, a certain EPC

```
 1 <soap:Envelope xmlns:soap="http://schemas.xmlsoap.org/soap/
     envelope/'>
 2  <soap:Body>
 3   <ns3:Poll xmlns:ns2="http://www.unece.org/cefact/
       namespaces/StandardBusinessDocumentHeader" xmlns:ns3="
       urn:epcglobal:epcis-query:xsd:1" xmlns:ns4="
       urn:epcglobal:epcis:xsd:1" xmlns:ns5="
       urn:epcglobal:epcis-masterdata:xsd:1'>
 4    <queryName>SimpleEventQuery</queryName>
 5    <params>
 6     <param>
 7      <name>GE_eventTime</name>
 8      <value xmlns:xs="http://www.w3.org/2001/XMLSchema"
         xmlns:xsi="http://www.w3.org/2001/XMLSchema-
         instance" xsi:type="xs:dateTime">2010-04-10
         T00:00:00Z</value>
 9     </param>
10     <param>
11      <name>EQ_action</name>
12      <value xmlns:xsi="http://www.w3.org/2001/XMLSchema-
         instance" xsi:type="ns3:ArrayOfString">
13       <string>OBSERVE</string>
14      </value>
15     </param>
16     <param>
17      <name>MATCH_epc</name>
18      <value xmlns:xsi="http://www.w3.org/2001/XMLSchema-
         instance" xsi:type="ns3:ArrayOfString">
19       <string>urn:epc:id:sgtin:1301757845.008.000133753170
         </string>
20      </value>
21     </param>
22    </params>
23   </ns3:Poll>
24  </soap:Body>
25 </soap:Envelope>
```

Listing A.3 SOAP: Simple event query result body containing filtered event data
for the query given in Listing A.2

```
 1 <soap:Envelope xmlns:soap=" http://schemas.xmlsoap.org/soap/
      envelope/"><soap:Body><ns3:QueryResults xmlns:ns2=" http://
      www.unece.org/cefact/namespaces/
      StandardBusinessDocumentHeader" xmlns:ns3="
      urn:epcglobal:epcis-query:xsd:1 " xmlns:ns4="
      urn:epcglobal:epcis:xsd:1 " xmlns:ns5=" urn:epcglobal:epcis-
      masterdata:xsd:1 ">
 2 <queryName>SimpleEventQuery</queryName>
 3 <resultsBody>
 4   <EventList>
 5     <ObjectEvent>
 6       <eventTime>2010-10-04T00:11:39.000+01:00</eventTime>
 7       <recordTime>2010-10-04T00:12:02.930+01:00</recordTime>
 8       <eventTimeZoneOffset>+01:00</eventTimeZoneOffset>
 9       <epcList><epc>urn:epc:id:sgtin:1301757845
            .008.000133753170</epc></epcList>
10       <action>OBSERVE</action>
11       <bizStep>urn:epcglobal:epcis:bizstep:fmcg:observe</
            bizStep>
12       <readPoint><id>urn:epc:id:sgln:1301757845.66446365.2</id
            ></readPoint>
13       <bizLocation><id>urn:epc:id:sgln:1301757845.66446365.2</
            id></bizLocation>
14     </ObjectEvent>
15     <ObjectEvent>
16       <eventTime>2010-10-04T16:01:53.000+01:00</eventTime>
17       <recordTime>2010-10-040T16:04:22.586+01:00</recordTime>
18       <eventTimeZoneOffset>+01:00</eventTimeZoneOffset>
19       <epcList><epc>urn:epc:id:sgtin:1301757845
            .008.000133753170</epc></epcList>
20       <action>OBSERVE</action>
21       <bizStep>urn:epcglobal:epcis:bizstep:fmcg:observe</
            bizStep>
22       <readPoint><id>urn:epc:id:sgln:549132542.340339831.2</id
            ></readPoint>
23       <bizLocation><id>urn:epc:id:sgln:549132542.340339831.2</
            id></bizLocation>
24     </ObjectEvent>
25   </EventList>
26 </resultsBody></ns3:QueryResults></soap:Body></soap:Envelope>
```

Listing A.4 ODRL: Request for the right to display eventdata for a certain EPC

```
1  <o:request type="o:request" uid="urn:policy:1296649173"
       xmlns:o="http://ordl.net/2.0">
2    <o:permission>
3      <o:action name="o:display"/>
4      <o:asset uid="urn:epc:id:sgtin:1318661593.003.000269655103
         "/>
5    </o:permission>
6  </o:request>
```

Listing A.5 ODRL: Response containing two permissions and one prohibition for displaying event data requested by the query given in Listing A.4

```
1  <o:policy type="o:set" uid="urn:policy:1296649173" xmlns:o="
       http://ordl.net/2.0">
2    <o:permission>
3      <o:action name="o:display"/>
4      <o:asset uid="urn:epc:id:sgln:1318661593.26806353"/>
5    </o:permission>
6    <o:permission>
7      <o:action name="o:display"/>
8      <o:asset uid="urn:epc:id:sgln:12"/>
9    </o:permission>
10   <o:prohibition>
11     <o:action name="o:display"/>
12     <o:asset uid="T1[0-5]:"/>
13   </o:prohibition>
14 </o:policy>
```

Table A.11 Costs distribution for RFID-enablement per supply chain role (I = Purely on-premise setup, II = Purely on-demand setup)

	Costs	A: Manufacturer		B: Wholesaler		E: Licensed Retailer	
	[EUR]	I	II	I	II	I	II
Hardware		28,906	17,988	15,339	9,880	7,929	2,470
RFID Writers	3,526	3x		–		–	
RFID Readers	913	6x		8x		2x	
Antennas	161	12x		16x		4x	
Workstations	3,261	2x	–	1x	–	1x	–
Servers	1,898	2x	–	1x	–	1x	–
Routers	300	2x	–	1x	–	1x	–
Software	908	6x	–	4x	–	2x	–
EPC Fees	2,650		1x		1x		1x
Implementation	400	400x	10x	350x	5x	250x	5x
Total [EUR]		197,004	24,638	161,621	14,530	112,395	7,120

Implementation costs have major impact on total costs. An on-demand setup is beneficial for wholesalers and retailers due to the reduced initial investments for hardware and implementation

A.6 Costs for RFID-Enablement Per Supply Chain Role

In the following, concrete costs for RFID-enablement per supply chain role are given; for evaluation please refer to Sect. 6.2.1.

References

1. B.W. Lampson, Protection, in *Proceedings of 5th Princeton Conference on Information Sciences and Systems*, pp. 437–443, 1971
2. D.F. Ferraiolo, D. Rick Kuhn, Role-based access control, in *Proceedings of the 15th NIST National Computer Security Conference*, pp. 554–563, 1992
3. G. Edjlali, A. Acharya, V. Chaudhary, History-based access control for mobile code, in *Proceedings of 5th Conference on Computer and Communications Security*, pp. 38–48, 1998
4. M. Abadi, C. Fournet, Access control based on execution history, in *Proceedings of the 10th Annual Network and Distributed System Security Symposium*, pp. 107–121, 2003
5. Oliver Günther, Sarah Spiekermann, RFID and the perception of control: the consumer's view. Commun. ACM **48**, 73–76 (2005)
6. S.L. Garfinkel, A. Juels, R. Pappu, RFID privacy: an overview of problems and proposed solutions. IEEE Secur. Priv. **3**, 34–43 (2005)
7. J. Song, T. Kim, S. Lee, H. Kim, Security enhanced RFID middleware system, in *World Academy of Science, Engineering and Technology*, pp. 79–82, 2005
8. M.I. Yagüe, Survey on XML-based policy languages for open environments. J. Inf. Assur. Secur. **1**(1), 11–20 (2006)
9. V.C. Hu, D.F. Ferraiolo, D. Rick Kuhn, Assessment of access control systems. Interagency Report 7316, National Institute of Standards and Technology, 2006
10. M.R. Rieback et al., A platform for RFID security and privacy administration, in *Proceedings of the Large Installation System Administration Conference*, pp. 89–102, Washington DC, USA, Dec. 2006

11. M.R. Rieback, B. Crispo, A.S. Tanenbaum, The evolution of RFID security. IEEE Pervasive Comput. **5**, 62–69 (2006)
12. Ari Juels, RFID security and privacy: a research survey. IEEE J. Sel. Areas Commun. **24**(2), 381–394 (2006)
13. T. Kim, H. Kim, Access control for middleware in RFID systems, in *Proceedings of the 8th International Conference on Advanced Communication Technology*, pp. 1020–1022, 2006
14. P. Peris-Lopez, J. C. Hernández Castro, J.M. Estévez-Tapiador, A. Ribagorda, RFID systems: a survey on security threats and proposed solutions, in *Proceedings of the 11th International Conference on Personal Wireless Communications, Lecture Notes in Computer Science*, vol. 4217 (Springer, Berlin, 2006), pp. 159 170
15. E. Grummt, M. Müller, R. Ackermann, Access control: challenges and approaches in the internet of things, in *Proceedings of the 2nd International Conference on WWW/Internet* (IADIS Press, Vila Real, Portugal, 2007), pp. 89–93
16. C. Groba, S. Groß, T. Springer, Context-dependent access control for contextual information, in *Proceedings of the 2nd International Conference on Availability, Reliability and Security*, Vienna, Austria, 4 Oct. 2007
17. B. King, X. Zhang, Securing the pharmaceutical supply chain using RFID, in *Proceedings of the International Conference on Multimedia and Ubiquitous Engineering* (IEEE Computer Society, Washington DC, 2007), pp. 23–28
18. B. Fabian, O. Günther, Distributed ONS and its impact on privacy, in *Proceedings of the International Conference on Communications*, pp. 1223–1228, 2007
19. S. Evdokimov, O. Günther, Practical access control management for outsourced EPC-related data in RFID-enabled supply chain, in *Proceedings of the International Conference on e-Business Engineering* (IEEE Computer Society, Washington DC, 2007), pp. 331–336
20. A. Ilic, F. Michahelles, E. Fleisch, The dual ownership model: using organizational relationships for access control in safety supply chains, in *Proceedings of the 21st International Conference on Advanced Information Networking and Applications Workshops*, vol. 2 (IEEE Computer Society, Washington DC, 2007), pp. 459–466
21. M. Langheinrich, RFID and privacy, in *Security, Privacy, and Trust in Modern Data Management*, Chap. 28, ed. by M. Petkovic, W. Jonker (Springer, Berlin, 2007), pp. 433–450
22. E. Grummt, M. Müller, Fine-grained access control for EPC information services, in *Proceedings of the 1st International Conference on Internet of Things*, pp 35–49, 2008
23. E. Grummt, M. Schöffel, Verteilte autorisation in RFID-ereignissystemen, in *D.A.C.H. Security—Bestandsaufnahme, Konzepte, Anwendungen, Perspektiven*, ed. by P. Horster, pp. 337–345, Berlin, Germany, 2008
24. P. Rotter, A framework for assessing RFID system security and privacy risks. IEEE Pervasive Comput. **7**, 70–77 (2008)
25. Q.Z. Sheng, X. Li, S. Zeadally, Enabling next-generation RFID applications: solutions and challenges. Computer **41**, 21–28 (2008)
26. M. Chung, J. Choi, S. Yang, S.-K. Rhyoo, Context-aware security services in DAA security model, in *Proceedings of the International Conference on Advanced Language Processing and Web Information Technology* (IEEE Computer Society, Washington DC, 2008), pp. 424–429
27. S. Spiekermann, S. Evdokimov, Critical RFID privacy-enhancing technologies. Comput. Sci. Eng. **7**, 56–62 (2009)
28. E. Grummt, A. Schill, Datensicherheit trotz transparenter Güterströme. Wissenschaftliche Zeitschrift der TU Dresden 103–107 (2009)
29. B. Fabian, O. Günther, Security challenges of the EPCglobal network. Commun. ACM **52**(7), 121–125 (2009)
30. B. Du, D. Wang, S. Ju, Access control for OSGi-based reconfigurable RFID middleware, in *Proceedings of the 4th International Conference on Computer Sciences and Convergence Information Technology* (IEEE Computer Society, Washington DC, 2009), pp. 1010–1014
31. A. Ilic, T. Andersen, F. Michahelles, Increasing supply-chain visibility with rule-based RFID data analysis. IEEE Internet Comput. **13**, 31–38 (2009)

32. X. Xia, S. Han, A privacy protection protocol for RFID-enabled supply chain system, in *Proceedings of the 6th International Conference on Services Systems and Services Management* (IEEE Computer Society, Washington DC, 2009), pages 305–308
33. Global Standards 1. EPCIS Standard 1.0.1. (2007), http://www.gs1.org/gsmp/kc/epcglobal/epcis/epcis_1_0_1-standard-20070921.pdf. Accessed 8 Mar 2012
34. ODRL Initiative. ODRL V2.0 - Common Vocabulary (2011), http://odrl.net/2.0/WD-ODRL-Vocab.html. Accessed 8 Mar 2012

Index

A
Access control, 13, 23
  discretionary, 13
  list, 14, 43
  matrix, 23
  non-discretionary, 14
  role-based, 14, 54, 75, 79
  rule-based, 16, 79
Anti-counterfeiting, 5, 18, 54, 92, 106
  service provider, 18, 43, 47, 109
  virtual product history, 4, 37, 42, 92
Attacks
  cloning, 37, 106
  distributed denial of service, 68, 88
  man-in-the-middle, 36 p, 68, 106
  replay, 38, 106
  spoofing, 37
Authentication, 61, 85
  mutual, 62
    dynamic, 64
    static, 62

C
Communication
  far Field, 19
  near Field, 19

D
Data, 32
  active, 57
  aging, 57
  availability, 32, 56
  confidentiality, 32
  integrity, 32 p, 61
  partitioning
    horizontal, 56

    range, 56
    round robin, 56
    vertical, 56
  passive, 57
  protection, 32
  quality, 33
  security, 32
  store
    column-oriented, 55
    insert-only, 55
    row-oriented, 54

E
Engineering
  design science methodology, 9
  software, 8
  system, 8
Enterprise applications
  customer relationship mgmt, 108
  enterprise resource planning, 17, 21, 108
  inventory management, 108
EPCglobal, 17
  application level events, 17
  certificate profile, 18, 21
  core business vocabulary, 17
  discovery conf. and initialization, 17
  EPC discovery services, 4, 17, 20
  EPC information services, 3, 17, 20 p, 54, 72, 106
  layers
    capture, 17
    exchange, 17
    identifcation, 17
  low level reader protocol, 17
  networks, 1, 3, 18, 61, 84, 105
  object name service, 17, 20, 85
  pedigree, 18

Matthieu-P. Schapranow, *Real-time Security Extensions for EPCglobal Networks*,
In-Memory Data Management Research, DOI: 10.1007/978-3-642-36343-6,
© Springer-Verlag Berlin Heidelberg 2014